Day Trading for a Living
5 Expert systems to Navigate the Stock Market

Book 1 of the DTL Series

Leigh Vernon

Copyright © 2018 by Leigh Vernon

All rights reserved.

No portion of this book may be reproduced in any form without written permission from the publisher or author, except as permitted by U.S. copyright law.

Contents

Introduction	1
Chapter 1: What You Should Know About Day Trading	2
Chapter 2: Secrets, Precautions, Necessities, Tips, And Points To Remember	10
Chapter 3: 10 Day Trading Tips to Become a Better Trader	15
Chapter 4: How to Develop a Profitable Day Trading System	19
Chapter 5: An Introduction To Candlestick Charts	24
Chapter 6: Trend Following: Moving Averages	39
Chapter 7: Trend Following: Cross-Over of Moving Averages	43
Chapter 8: Trend Following - Turtle Trading	45
Chapter 9: Counter-Trend Following - Williams %R	48
Chapter 10: Counter-Trend Following - Relative Strength Index	51
Chapter 11: How Much Money Is Required To Start Day Trading?	54
Chapter 12: The Secrets to Day Trading Success	66
Chapter 13: The Seven Fundamentals for Day Trading	68
Chapter 14: Dispelling the Myths of Day-Trading	86
Conclusion	89
Check Out Other Books	90

Introduction

The day trading business is as predictable as the weather. There are highs and lows that occur within hours, even minutes and seconds from each other. Day trading is essentially defined as the buying and selling of a security – a negotiable financial instrument that holds some type of monetary value. What makes it even more interesting and challenging is the trade occurs in the same day, in a span of hours, minutes, or even seconds. Most day tradings can occur in the foreign exchange rate and stock market. Day traders contribute to keeping the market running efficiently by providing liquidity and arbitrage.

However, it is important to note that this book does not guarantee that you can make giant profits or provide sure-win methods in trading. Instead, it is assumed that you have already engaged in day trading activities, and are on the hunt for proven strategies to polish your existing ones, or to replace them. As a day trader, all the rules you have learned about finding good stocks over the years won't matter. Day trading is a completely different game with its own set of rules, but if you know what you are doing you will be able to fine-tune strategies that work best for you.

This book will help guide you to become the day trader you want to be. It may not happen automatically and all at once, but making money is possible if you put in the time, effort, commitment, and dedication it demands.

Chapter 1: What You Should Know About Day Trading

The Day Trader

A day trader can be two things: a risk manager and a hunter of volatility. Simply put, the job of a day trader is one who buys shares of a certain stock and sells it within a number of minutes or hours in order to gain a profit. This is why day traders look for volatility in such a short period of time. This is influenced by any of these three things: companies that have just released news, reported earnings, or other reasons that increase public interest. All these things influence how a day trader chooses to enter and exit a particular stock or share.

There are two types of day traders. The first one is a professional who works for large financial institutions. Some will say that this is the best place for you to start because you will most likely have a mentor – and several other professionals – guiding you on how to do the tricks of the trade. You will have access to tools and the latest technology to help you analyse your strategies. With this arrangement, you will be paid a basic salary and occasionally a bonus. Perhaps the best take-away with this is you won't be using your own money to trade, saving you the risk of time and money, while enjoying employee benefits.

The second type is called the individual trader. Armed with the ability to understand technical analysis and how the market works in a thorough sense, they trade for themselves. They also have a large quantity of money to invest in, mainly because the gains will be miniscule if you only invest a small amount. These are the people who have learned to define their own trading style through experience.

What makes a good day trader? Many theories surround this topic, with a number of conflicting and opposing views. Even if two individuals start with the same capital, the same trading platform, and the same trading systems with the same entry and exit points, the results can still be different. So what the key difference that sets them apart? It's not about intelligence, inherent talent, or even dedication and focus. Both people want to succeed, so why does one enjoy a profit while the other one suffers loss?

In a book by American psychologist Dr. Van Tharp, he discussed the role of psychology in trading – and it's much more significant than you think. In a pie chart he calls the "Ingredients of Trading", he divides three aspects – system, management, and psychology. System accounted for 10% of the pie, with Management next on the list at 30%. Interestingly, psychology clocked in at 60% - the biggest part of the pie that accounts for the top influencer and difference in the styles of day traders. But what exactly is this psychology he was referring to, and how can it help us become better day traders?

In a nutshell, psychology refers to your emotions, feelings, thoughts, and actions that affect your investment decisions. Day trading in the stock market makes it possible for you to gain profit and lessen risk, but emotions often play a huge influence on how you react and handle different situations. Take for example the day trader who is prone to react emotionally, and in the end makes various wrong decisions.

He keeps holding on to a losing position, with the belief that it will turn out to be a winner – someday. This classic mistake has a name to it and it is called loss aversion. It is the tendency for people to defer likely gains by holding on tight and avoiding losses. Even with the market spiralling downward, loss aversion keeps traders from letting go and cutting off losses. What is even more interesting is that traders of this nature usually display signs of other irrational behaviour. An example of this is attributing success to exceptional trading skills and losses to bad timing and bad luck. Without controlling your emotions, you will lose money very quickly in the markets. This is because you are reacting on impulse and holding on to strong beliefs that can be damaging to your portfolio.

If emotions play a large part in determining whether you will succeed or fail in day trading, how then can we change our psychology? How can we shift our focus and learn to manage and keep our emotions under control? How can we keep a cool and rational head in order to be more receptive to the fluctuations in the market?

The answer lies in discipline. A successful day trader never rests on his own laurels. He knows that he's never reached the peak of his skills and abilities just yet, despite past successes. He makes conscious and deliberate choices when making decisions, until this ability develops muscle memory. Discipline then, can be trained, when practiced daily and deliberately.

Another important skill in order to be a successful day trader is to develop your own set of trading rules. This should guide you on when to enter or exit a stock. Over time, and after accumulating years of experience and trying out different strategies, you will soon reach a point where you find a comfortable and effective way to trade.

Once you find the sweet spot that works for you, stick to it, improve it, and implement it. Lastly, keep your emotions in check at all times. Having self-control can make you immune to the highs and lows of trading, and help keep your cool through the downturn, panic, or euphoria that occurs during day trading. Learn to accept losses with grace and move on to the next one.

Over time, you will learn that you will inevitably lose without discipline. You may have the right skills but when you allow greed and fear to start taking control over your decisions, you will not succeed. The most important thing to ask yourself here is whether you have the commitment to remain disciplined, as discipline can be learned.

Your Trading Strategy

At 11:10 am, a day trader might buy 1,000 shares on McDonald's stocks just when prices begin to increase due to the release of good news. The day trader then decides to sell the stock at 11:20 am when the stocks climb up by $1 per share. With this, he can easily make $1,000 in just 10 minutes. How does he do it?

A great day trader accepts that each trade he makes has its own level of risk, and he adheres to a specific set of rules set for that trade. This is called trading strategy. It includes rules in defining when to enter and to exit, based on certain conditions, trade triggers, timeframe, management of money and financials, and other relevant and useful information. It also includes historical data based on previous trends and performance in order to project future performance.

When a trading strategy is properly executed, it can give you a mathematical expectation for how to determine if a certain trade is really profitable or not. While trading strategies aren't free from limitations, it does provide a risk-adjusted return, which may or may not guarantee success on your part. They are a great way to avoid financial biases and help to secure consistent results over a long period of time.

The success rate of day traders is estimated to be only around 10%, with a whopping 90% losing money. And top of this, only 1% really make serious profit. By definition, if you are buying, then there must be someone selling. With this analogy, then there must be someone making money, while the other one loses money. This is why trading strategies are the backbone of any day trader. Without a properly designed one, you will be heading into battle without a helmet on.

While the importance of trading strategies cannot be over-emphasised, the downside is that they are difficult to develop. It's easy to become reliant on one strategy, but it does not ensure that you will get the same positive result at all times. While there are some methodologies with a ready set of rules handed down to us, there will come a time when you must devise your very own.

Your system has to reflect who you are. But despite the differences, and seemingly opposing sets of rules for different day trading strategies, only one thing is common – the system needs to be systematic. Regardless of how unique your circumstances are, putting in place a defined system can strap you in for the long-term. When designing your own system, ask yourself of the following questions:

- Is my system designed for capital growth or cash flow?
- Am I trading part-time or full-time?
- How much money can I afford to lose?
- What percentage of annual rate am I aiming for?

Analysing Trading Systems

There are systems that buy on strength and sell on weakness, while others do the exact opposite. Some may make their millions through momentum trading; others are more comfortable as value investors. Despite the fact that there are many methods, there are countless ways to gain profit as well.

If a trading strategy works in a system, then there has to be several parts that constitute to it as a whole. Typically, a trading system has the following:

- Selecting your market
- Selecting your time frame
- Selecting a trading style
- Defining entry points

- Defining exit points
- Evaluation
- Improving your trading strategy

In order to understand different trading systems, we need to take a look at these parts individually.

Selecting Your Market

Financial instruments in recent times have allowed private investors to have a variety of choices in trading. In addition, these have also been enhanced by virtue of the introduction of electronic contracts that make it easier to access shares and stocks. For example, you can invest in real estate investment fund without even owning a property. These days, traders have the option to trade anything amid everything available to them.

The four main markets include stocks, Forex, futures, and stock options. As only stocks and Forex are primarily used in day trading, only these two will be discussed.

The stock market can be a public or private market that is used for the trading of a company stock on an agreed price. When a company makes itself available on the stock market, it is given a value by investors, wherein the value of the company is divided into what we know as shares.

You, as a day trader, can have the capacity to buy and sell these shares in return, making you a shareholder of a company for a certain time. The value of the company can increase or decrease, bringing the value of your bought shares along with it.

When the company makes a profit, you may receive some of that profit in the form of dividends. This profit is divided amongst everyone who owns shares in the company. While stocks markets usually have good volatility and liquidity, the requirements for initial capital are usually high.

The second market in focus is Forex, which is the abbreviation of the term Foreign Exchange. Just like any other form of trading, it follows the basic rule of buying when the market is going up, and selling when it is going down. The only difference is that with Forex trading, the day trader buys and sells currencies. In simpler terms, it's the exchange of currency at an agreed upon rate for another currency.

All currencies are automatic participants in this trade, but just as there are blue chips stocks, there are also currencies that stand out as more powerful ones than all others. The top five are the US dollar, the Japanese Yen, the British Pound, the Swiss Franc, and the European Union Euro.

Take note that you will always need to trade currencies in pairs, buying one currency while simultaneously selling another. Because it requires only a small amount of capital and less emotional investment, Forex trading can be a great start to polish your trading skills to prepare you for higher and more difficult markets.

Selecting Your Time Frame

Day trading time frames are set only within a particular day, but intraday timeframes can range as low as 1 minute or as high as 60 minutes, perhaps even more. With smaller timeframes, the average profit is usually low, but in exchange, you get higher trading opportunities. The opposite occurs when you trade in a larger timeframe – the average profit will be bigger, but there will be fewer chances to trade. If you're just starting out, it is better to try trading in smaller timeframes at first.

This way, you can prevent over-leveraging your account and have minimal associated risk. The only problem with too short timeframes is that you can encounter a lot of distractions and short manipulated moves that you can mistake for an emerging trend. This is why the ideal timeframe is 15 minutes. It is small enough for intraday moves, and large enough to establish trends and reduce "noise".

Selecting a Trading Style

Trading systems can generally be broken down into technical strategies and fundamental strategies. Both can be tested on accuracy because they rely on quantifiable information. The main difference is that with technical strategies, the day trader relies on generating technical signals from technical indicators, while fundamental strategies consider fundamental factors into account. For example, a technical trading strategy may involve the use of a moving-average cross-over; in the fundamental arena, the investor looks at other specific criteria like revenue or growth to evaluate his opportunity.

By definition, fundamental stock analysis requires the day trader to take a close examination of financial statements of the company. The day trader will then most likely estimate whether the stocks are undervalued or overvalued, by virtue of the company's current financial strength, current management skills, future growth, and profitability prospects. Annual and quarterly reports are given importance as well as any news or rumours about the company.

On the other hand, the premise of technical analysis lies in the understanding that patterns tend to repeat themselves and tend to follow a certain direction. It involves the study of stocks with the use of charts, graphs, support and resistance levels, trendlines, and other mathematical tools which will help the day trader establish and predict future movements in order to identify opportunities.

Defining Entry Points

Because the market is constantly moving, you need to be able to identify entry points and make decisions at the speed of lightning. It all sounds complicated at first, but the skills needed for this can be learned. When deciding when to enter, practice identifying the entry rules of your chosen strategy. If you know your selected approach very well, learn its own rules.

Make sure you understand the market condition and select the best strategy that is most suited for that trend. Don't worry about exit points just yet – focus on getting an entry first, as stipulated by the rules of your chosen system.

Defining Exit Points

Now you have come to the most important crux of trading. Here are three points you need to know in order to exit effectively:

- ***Stop loss***

This is defined as the limit used to prevent the loss form being too damaging when the trade goes against you. If you don't apply stop losses in your trading, chances are you will be losing a lot of your capital. The trick here is for you to make a set of rules and stick to those rules no matter what. Know when the right time is for you to cut a losing position before entering a trade.

Once you've entered a trade, place a stop at once. This ensures you won't be losing all of your money. Remember, profit is far more important than pride. Admit defeat when your trade backfires and exit in order to lessen the opportunity cost, and use the remaining freed capital elsewhere to fight back.

- ***Profit taking exits***

Once you begin seeing profits in your trade, it can be very tempting to sit back and ride the wave as much as you can before making an exit. Human beings are by nature greedy, and this can often contribute to their downfall. Instead of taking huge profits on a single trade, try to take smaller profits consistently instead. The easiest to do this would be to specify a target profit and exit when it is achieved.

- ***Time stops***

While the first two exit strategies require you to set stop losses and profit exit points, exiting on these pre-determined values, Time Stops allow you to decide on your exit only after you entered a trade. This strategy requires your full attention to the emerging trends in your trade, and this is where technical analysis can be of great help.

An example of a good time stop is three times the time-frame you're using. If you are using charts of 15-minute timeframes, consider abandoning the trade if you have not reached your target within 45 minutes. Your entry might be wrong if nothing happens after a certain time.

Now that you've familiarized yourself with the different aspects of trading, we can now take a look at some day trading systems you can use in the subsequent chapters.

Chapter 2: Secrets, Precautions, Necessities, Tips, And Points To Remember

Day trading-Buying and selling of shares on daily basis is called day trading. This is also called intra-day trading. Whatever you buy/sell, you have to buy/sell on the same day, and very importantly during the market opening hours.

Advantages of Day Trading

a) Margin trading - In Day trading you get a margin on your balance amount which means you get more leverage on your available balance. This concept is called margin trading. Margin trading is only possible in day trading and not in delivery trading. How much extra amount (margin) you are going to get that totally depends on your broker, or your online system brokers.

Some broker provides 3, 4, 5, and 6 times extra margin. If you do margin then you have to square off your open trades on the same day (means if you bought shares then you have to sell and if you sold shares then you have to buy)before market time (that is 3:30 PM) finishes.b)

Second important advantage is that you have to pay is less brokerage (commissions) on day trading (Intraday) as compared to delivery trading. This brokerage again depends from broker to broker (or on your online trading system). c) In day trading you can sell and then buy this is called short sell which you cant do in delivery trading. You can sell shares when prices are falling and then buy when price falls further.

Disadvantages of Day Trading

a) As you are benefited to get more extra amount to trade (that is margin trading) and get more extra profit it is also equally true that you are also taking more risk of loss.b) At any cost you have to square off the open transaction before 3:30 PM (especially if you are doing margin trading) at that time the price may not be in your favor.

Basic Requirements for Day trading

A successful day trader or share market trading requires couple of disciplines and following requirements -

1) PC with internet - If you need to do it yourself then you need to have a PC or else you can do it in internet café also. A PC with good internet connection speed. The internet connection should not be slow or should not face any other problem especially in Day Trading.

2) Online Account (Demat Account) - You need to open online share trading account with any of the available banks or online brokers. Points to remember while opening online account) Make multiple enquiries and try get low brokerage trading and demat account.b) Also discuss about the margin they provide for day trading. c) Discuss about fund transfer.

The fund transfer should be reliable and easy. Fund transfer from your bank account to account and visa versa. Some online share accounts have integrated savings account which makes easy for you to transfer funds from your saving account to trading account.d) Very important is about service they provide, the research calls, intraday or daily tips. e) Also enquire about their services charges and any other hidden charges if any. f) And also see how reliable and easy is to contact them in case if any emergency. Emergency closing or squaring off trades in case of any technical or other problems

How to choose shares (stocks) for day trading

In day trading, traders mostly wish to do buying and selling on small profits or else they look for overbought or oversold shares. Taking into consideration these important points following basic things you should look in for shares while choosing them for day trading.- Price Volatility- Volume (quantity)What exactly these terms mean and how to use them while Day Trading.

Price Volatility - The Price volatility means the movement (up and down) of share price should be more (or high) through out the day. In other words the fluctuation in share prices should be on high rate so that it will be easy for you to buy and sell on different prices. Suppose if share is moving up and down in very narrow range then on what price you will buy and sell? So it is always better if you choose shares which have high volatility in price movement.Do you want to know how to find out the high volatility shares then please click here?

Volume (quantity) - Volume means trading quantities. The shares which you choose for day trading should have high volumes (or high traded quantity).Why this is required?The high volume indicates that there is more liquidity. Liquidity means lots of transactions had took place on this share and more people are interested to trade in this share. This will ease your trading job because you will get more exposure to the price to buy and sell at anytime. Due to high volumes there will be also high price fluctuations.

Points to remember for day tradingFollowing are very important points to be always remember by day traders.Entry & exit points, stop loss limits, profit targets, your desired risk/reward profile,amount of capital to be committed to trades, how long you need to hold the share if incase it is against your favor.

Why it is required to practice day trading before starting actual day trading?

It's important to do practice or paper trading before you starts actual trading. Following are the few reasons, 1) Very importantly you will come to know how to place buy/sell orders, and will become familiar and perfect about using your trading system. 2) You will gain confidence in yourself. 3) The fear of trading will vanish. It is very important to keep fear away while doing day trading. 4) You will become active to enter and exit the trade. It's vital important that you must be pretty fast to enter and exit the trade (i.e. open positions).

What are the common day trading mistakes and how to avoid them to make generous profit

1) Don't jump in trend early - Wait and get paper confirmation of trend change, and then plan and do your trades (buy/sell). Don't jump in or do early trades before any trade change confirmation this may damage your capital (bank balance).

2) Don't wait in trade for long time - Suppose that you had done one trade (either buy or sell) but the scrip is not moving either up or down, it is just stable or moving with very low price difference, then you should get out of that trade and look for other scrip's.

You may encounter these type of situations when indices (NSE or BSE) and not moving (or moving with narrow range). At such time either you wait or come out of trade, don't loose patience and fall under loss.

3) Don't change your trend on volume volatility - Some time you enter in trade by seeing the buy and sell quantities. For example, suppose you brought shares by seeing more buy quantity then sell quantity, expecting more buy quantity may push the share/stock up but after few minutes you see exactly reverse that you see more sell quantity and less buy quantity or both buy and sell high quantity or the difference of buying and selling quantity is decreased as compared to what you had seen before.

So this point is very important, don't panic here and sell off your stock, wait and realize the situation properly and then take action. This situation comes many times but if you are sure that your share is going to move up then stick to it.

4) Beware of companies' acquisition or any announcement by Government - Suppose in the morning, before market begins, you should read or viewed the news of any Indian Company has acquired any foreign company (or part of foreign company) if you see this is actually best news/things that Indian company. But if acquisition amount is far more than expectation then this good news will turn into worst news. The shares of that company will start falling.

So you should not get in trade and buy shares you have to wait and watch how market or other people are responding to these shares and once you understand then you can trade. So always watch where the market heading towards and then react. Announcement of Government - You should also be very careful to decide your tarde based on any government announcement.

For example, if government has declared any hike in interest rate then its good news for bank stocks and hence the shares will rise but if government has declared 2nd rate hike in very less span of time as company to first one (stay within duration of one, two month or three month) then this news will be worse for bank stocks, the share may keeping fall during the trading period. So realize and analyze the news and finally watch market behavior and this fall or do trade you will get success.

Things to study in the morning before starting your day trading or share market trading or Intraday trading?

1) Read financial newspaper like Business Standard, Economics Times, etc. If possible note done the high lights/breaking news with respective company names and keep close watch on them for that day.

2) If possible watch share (stock) market related TV channels like Zee Business, CNBC, etc. In these TV channels you get over all idea/movements of all share prices and markets (BSE, NSE). And also it becomes easy to catch and keep close watch on related companies if any breaking news comes out during that day.

3) Especially some share market related websites like capitalmarket.com, businessstandard.com always displays current news, market affairs, share market trends, breaking news and various announcement done by company or government which may effect the share market and related companies. So try to access and have all OK on such types of websites before starting trading and also through out the day, if possible.

4) So in short before starting you stock market trading you should be well aware of all the current news of financial market and if possible note down the breaking news or effective news and its related company and keep watch on that share and trade accordingly on that day.

Important principles to be follow by day tradersNever invest all your money in same sector this method is called as diversification of shares. This will protect your money from downtrends of any particular sector as you can make money from other sector.There are various sectors like IT, Pharmacy, Banking, Steel, Petrol and Oil, construction and infrastructure, auto etc.

Avoid common day trading mistakes Lack of a Trading Plan, Failure to Control Emotions, Failure to Accept and Limit Losses, Lack of Commitment, Over-Trading

Chapter 3: 10 Day Trading Tips to Become a Better Trader

Warren Buffett once said, "The stock market is a device for transferring money from the impatient to the patient." This applies to both - traders and investors alike. However, if you are an absolute beginner, there is always some room for improvement. We have listed below the 10 best day trading tips that successful traders follow. Learn them mindfully and take note to level up your trading. Moreover, you can also check out the best day trading tips and make money from online trading in Indian stock markets.

This is why rookie traders often look for advice from experts who have carved their names in the industry. Read on to find out what you may require before venturing in this high-risk but ultimately-rewarding industry.

Learn from a Professional Trader - Day Trading Tips

It is always better to learn to trade from an expert before you jump directly into the ocean. Try and find out who has a good teaching methodology and carefully choose the one that suits your style. Most of the trainers or masters will definitely charge a fee for the time spared. Don't you worry! It is no fee. It is called investment.

After all, you are a trader and one day when you have made it big, you may be approached by newbies and you likewise charge them. But most importantly, if you invest into education, you are saving on market tuition from learning the lessons the hard way, on the expense of your account balance.

Pay Attention to the Financial News

Want to be the best trader around? Keep a close eye on the world around you especially business news. Stay updated about firms entangled in IP issues, Failed FDA nod, Board reshuffle, International projects, and dismal earnings estimates of the quarter.

Every news related to the firm you are making an investment in makes sense. Back your decision with these inputs. For a smarter decision while trading, keep abreast of every piece of information on your preferred investment firm.

Found Your Niche? Ace It!

Nobody can guarantee you a blockbuster return. You make your own choices and decisions and learn from your mistakes. Only you know which strategies or niches worked for you and which don't. If you really have the zeal to excel in day trading, you need to be right on top of your business.

Once you have found the niche to work upon, become really good at that. Master it and it will enhance your odds of success in the trading manifold.

Treat it like a Business!

Have a hobby? Pursue it somewhere else. Making money and day trading is a serious business. You don't do it for fun so even before you start to trade, you need to settle with the fact that it is a serious, time-consuming business and it will take time to break even. If you want to gamble, Las Vegas might have better odds.

Follow the Pros

Julius Caesar once said, "Experience is the teacher of all things." Trading experts, despite their level of training, have a lot to boast, thanks to experience.

Follow the moves of the pros and find out what are they investing in? When do they buy? When do they sell? For how long do they hold? Try and understand how profit is made. You can learn a great deal from the mistakes they once made and then harness them to your advantage.

Have Patience

Rome was not built in a day. It takes time to master any skill and the same goes with stock trading. It can give you the best returns only if you trade wisely. Researchers have shown that those who trade less tend to earn better than the one who trades very frequently.

This is just like stalking your prey and then striking when you have absolute chances of success. Always remember that when you trade in average and not-so-good setups, you lose on good deals and eventually your profits take a hit. Therefore, one crucial day trading tips are that quality matters over quantity.

Don't be Emotional & Follow Day Trading Tips

The world of trading calls that you keep a level mind and remember that if you let your emotions get the better of you while trading, you will most likely lose out on your money. Emotions make you take irrational, impulsive decisions which should never happen.

Frequent errors like letting your losses get out of proportion, adding to a losing position, not making timely withdrawals et cetera are made time and again. People fall into the emotional trap and make unconsidered decisions. And while you cannot help having them, learning to control your emotions will go a long way in positioning you as a shrewd trader. Work on the emotional quotient and you'll make wiser decisions.

Sharing is Caring

Now that you have learned from your mistakes and other's as well, it is time to share. You must share the experience you had while trading. You can start a blog, a YouTube channel or other medium for reaching out. Furthermore, you can have a comment section for answering the questions of your visitors.

This will not only help others but will certainly keep you disciplined. This habit will make you more accountable and you might think twice before making a trade you know, you should not be making.

When There Are No Good Plays, Don't Trade!

What? Do not be shocked as this is no less a practical tip than the rest. Sometimes it is good that you don't trade. Trading just for the mere fact is not a smart choice.

Trade only when you see money lying on the floor or the offer is too lucrative to let it go. Take your chances and remember that this is a highly dynamic world so weigh all possible benefits of making a move against sitting back and speculating.

Have Confidence

As obvious as it may sound, this is a key component of a refined trader. Whichever trading style you choose, you got to believe in yourself as failure to believe in the efforts you are putting or the decisions you are taking will never make you a winner. I might sound strange but people do not get good returns just because they cannot believe they will. This negative thinking results in negative returns.

Remember! Successful traders were also amateurs and novices when they started out. Their success has come from the hard work and efforts they have put in. Make mistakes and learn from them to continue trading until you start making profits.

As mentioned in the beginning, these day trading tips shared will let you learn some important hacks to improve Your game. Apply these diligently and you are sure to advance in your endeavors.

Chapter 4: How to Develop a Profitable Day Trading System

In this part I will explain to you how to develop a profitable day trading system in five steps.

Step 1: Select a market and a timeframe

Every market and every timeframe can be traded with a day trading system. But if you want to look at 50 different futures markets and 6 major timeframes (e.g. 5min, 10min, 15min, 30min, 60min and daily), then you need to evaluate 300 possible options. Here are some hints on how to limit your choices:

- Though you can trade every futures markets, we recommend that you stick to the electronic markets (e.g. e-mini S&P and other indices, Treasury Bonds and Notes, Currencies, etc). Usually these markets are very liquid, and you won't have a problem entering and exiting a trade. Another advantage of electronic markets is lower commissions: Expect to pay at least half the commissions you pay on non-electronic markets. Sometimes the difference can be as high as 75%.

- When you select a smaller timeframes (less than 60min) your average profit per trade is usually comparably low. On the other hand you get more trading opportunities. When trading on a larger timeframe your profits per trade will be bigger, but you will have less trading opportunities. It's up to you to decide which timeframe suits you best.

- Smaller timeframes mean smaller profits, but usually smaller risk, too. When you are starting with a small trading account, then you might want to select a small timeframe to make sure that you are not overtrading your account.

Most profitable day trading systems use larger timeframes like daily and weekly. These systems work, too, but, be prepared for less trading action and bigger drawdowns.

Step 2: Define entry rules

Let's simplify the myths of "entry rules":

Basically there are 2 different kinds of entry setups:

- Trend-following

When prices are moving up, you buy, and when prices are going down, you sell.

- Trend-fading

When prices are trading at an extreme (e.g. upper band of a channel), you sell, and you try to catch the small move while prices are moving back into "normalcy." The same applies for selling.

In my opinion swing trading is actually one of the best trading strategies for the beginning trader to get his or her feet wet. By contrast, trend trading offers greater profit potential if a trader is able to catch a major market trend of weeks or months, but few are the traders with sufficient discipline to hold a position for that period of time without getting distracted.

Most indicators that you will find in your charting software belong to one of these two categories: You have either indicators for identifying trends (e.g. Moving Averages) or indicators that define overbought or oversold situations and therefore offer you a trade setup for a short-term swing trade.

So don't become confused by all the possibilities of entering a trade. Just make sure that you understand why you are using a certain indicator or what the indicator is measuring. An example of a simple swing daytrading strategy can be found in the next chapter.

Step 3: Define exit rules

Let's keep it simple here, too: There are two different exit rules you want to apply:

- Stop Loss Rules to protect your capital and
- Profit Taking Exits to realize your profits

Both exit rules can be expressed in four ways:

- A fixed dollar amount (e.g. $1,000)
- A percentage of the current price (e.g. 1% of the entry price)

- A percentage of the volatility (e.g. 50% of the average daily movement) or
- A time stop (e.g. exit after 3 days)

We don't recommend using a fixed dollar amount, because markets are too different. For example, natural gas changes an average of a few thousand dollars per day per contract; however, Eurodollars change an average of a few hundred dollars a day per contract. You need to balance and normalize this difference when developing a day trading system and testing it on different markets. That's why you should always use percentages for stops and profit targets (e.g. 1% stop) or a volatility stop instead of a fixed dollar amount.

A time stop gets you out of a trade if it is not moving in any direction, therefore freeing your capital for other trades.

Step 4: Evaluate your day trading system

The first figure to look for is the net profit. Obviously you want your system to generate profits. But don't be frustrated when during the development stage your day trading system shows a loss; try to reverse your entry signals. You already learned that trading is a zero sum game: So if you are going long at a certain price level, and you lose, then try to go short instead. Many times this is the easiest way to turn a losing system into a winning one.

The next figure you want to look at is the average profit per trade. Make sure this number is greater than slippage and commissions, and that it makes your day trading worthwhile. Day trading is all about risk and reward, and you want to make sure you get a decent reward for your risk.

Take a look at the Profit Factor (Gross Profit / Gross Loss). This will tell you how many dollars you are likely to win for every dollar you lose. The higher the profit factor the better the day trading system. A system should have a profit factor of 1.5 or more, but watch out when you see profit factors above 3.0, because it might be that you over-optimized the system.

Here are some more characteristics you might want to consider besides the net profit of a system:

Winning percentage

Many profitable day trading systems achieve a nice net profit with a rather small winning percentage, sometimes even below 30%. These systems follow the principle "Cut your losses short and let your profits run." However, YOU need to decide whether you can stand 7 losers and only 3 winners in 10 trades. If you want to be "right" most of the time, then you should pick a system with a high winning percentage.

Number of Trades per Month

Do you need daily action? If you want to see something happening every day, then you should pick a day trading system with a high number of trades per month. Many profitable day trading systems generate only 2-3 trades per month, but if you are not patient enough to wait for it, then you should select a day trading system with a higher trading frequency.

Average Time in Trade

Some people get really nervous when they are in a trade. I have heard of people who can't even sleep at night when they have an open position. If that's you, then you should make sure that the average time in a trade is as short as possible. You might want to choose a system that does not hold any positions overnight.

Maximum Drawdown

A famous trader once said: "If you want your system to double or triple your account, you should expect a drawdown of up to 30% on your way to trading riches." Not every trader can stand a 30% drawdown. Look at the maximum drawdown the system produced so far, and double it. If you can stand this drawdown, then you found the right day trading system. Why doubling? Remember: your worst drawdown is always ahead of you.

Most consecutive losses

The amount of most consecutive losses has a huge impact on your trading, especially when you are using certain types of money management techniques. Five or six consecutive losses can cause you a lot of trouble when using an aggressive money management.

In addition this number will help you to determine whether you have enough discipline to trade the system: Will you still trade the system after you have experienced 10 losses in a row? It's not unusual for a profitable trading system to have 10-12 losses in a row.

Step 5: Improving your system

There is a difference between "improving" and "curve-fitting" a system. You can improve your day trading system by testing different exit methods: If you are using a fixed stop, try a trailing stop instead. Add a time stop and evaluate the results again. Don't look at the net profit only; look also at the profit factor, average profit per trade and maximum drawdown. Many times you will see that the net profit slightly decreases when you add different stops, but the other figures might improve dramatically.

Don't fall into the trap of over-optimizing: You can eliminate almost all losers by adding enough rules. Simple example: If you see that on Tuesdays you had more losers than on the other weekdays, you might be tempted to add a "filter" that prevents your day trading system from entering trades on Tuesdays. Next you find that in January you had much worse results than in other months, so you add a filter that enters trades only from February - December. You add more and more filters to avoid losses, and eventually you end up with a trading rule that I saw recently:

IF FVE > -1 And Regression Slope (Close , 35) / Close.35 * 100 > -.35 And Regression Slope (Close , 35) / Close.35 * 100 -.4 And Regression Slope (Close , 70) / Close.70 * 100 -.2 And MACD Diff (Close , 12 , 26 , 9) > -.003 And Not Tuesday And Not DayOfMonth = 12 and not Month = August and Time > 9:30 ...

Though you eliminated all possibilities of losing (in the past) and this trading system is now producing fantastic profits, it's very unlikely that it will continue to do so when it hits reality.

Chapter 5: An Introduction To Candlestick Charts

It's hard to believe that Japanese candlestick charts were almost completely unknown in the West, before being introduced in 1989 by a American called Steve Nison in his book entitled Japanese Candle Charting Techniques. These techniques are now so widely used throughout the financial industry, it is hard to imagine a world without them.

What is unique is that a simple candle shape can hold so much information, but because it is graphically and colourfully displayed it allows the mind to absorb information very quickly. Combined with our knowledge of volume, they provide the two elements that will form the basis of your trading. As you will have guessed they are called candles or candlesticks because that is what they look like!

Each Candlestick has FOUR elements as follows, namely an opening price, a low price, a high price and a closing price within the time frame being considered. Where the price has closed up in the time period then these are generally coloured blue, and where the price has closed down they are generally show as red.

The reason they are so powerful is because they show instantly and visually the price movements over a certain period. As you will learn later, all aspects of the candle are important, but particularly the size of the body, the length of the wicks (upper and lower) and of course whether it is an up or down candle.

Now that you understand the basic formation of a candlestick I am going to discuss timescales in a little more detail. It may surprise you to know that on my currency trading charts I have the following timescales : 5 seconds, 10 seconds, 30 seconds, 1 minute, 5 min, 10 min, 15 min,30 min and onwards to the monthly.

The reason I mention it now is firstly to make you aware that you can have candlestick charts in virtually any timeframe you like (all charting packages are slightly different), and secondly if you are not careful, you will spend your time like some lost soul endless flicking between timeframes to try to look for confirmation of something you have seen in another timeframe!

Don't worry, everyone has the same problem when they start, it is part of human nature! Every form of trading has different requirements and in addition this also depends on the length of time you are going to be holding positions open. Let me try to give a silly example, which I hope will make the point.

As I mentioned it above, take the 5 second charts as an example. Imagine you were buying shares as part of your investment portfolio for the next few years. You would not base your decision on a 5 second chart would you! (no you wouldn't!! - really you wouldn't) The timescale of your holding and the timescale of chart you are looking at are completely out of balance with one another. You would look at a daily, weekly or even monthly chart going back several years. The timescales are relevant to one another and you must base your decision on a relevant chart for the time you are likely to be holding the trade.

Now let's look at another trade using the 5 second chart. In currency trading you have people who trade by what's called scalping. In the currency markets the prices move around constantly and sometimes very fast indeed. In a few seconds a price may have moved several points. A scalper will trade large amounts of money on small movements, trading in and out of the markets several hundred times a day. There would be little point looking at an hourly or daily chart. Trading would be over by the time you pushed the button. A silly example I know, but I hope you get the point. Scalpers would use anything between 10 second and 5 minutes, and in case you're wondering, no I am not a scalper nor do I ever look at these timescales. My trades are longer term hours, days and sometimes weeks, so I use hourly and daily charts 95% of the time (much less stressful)

Finally, let my try to give you four generalizations for the candles themselves (I'll call them candles from now on as it is less typing!) which I hope will give you some very basic guidance. Remember there are whole books and websites dedicated to the study and analysis of candle charts and you will have to do lots of reading, study and practice to become expert, but in general the following are true:

1. The longer the body of the candle then the more meaningful the move & the more volume(effort) required.

2. It takes effort to go down as well as up so 1 applies whether it is an up or a down candle.

3. The longer the wick on the candle (top or bottom) then the more one can interpret from the candle.

4. When a candle has the open and close price very close together this represents indecision in the market.

5. The same candle can mean different things depending on where it appears in the overall chart

6. You never act on one candle alone, but wait for confirmation in the next few bars.

Now whatever time frame you are trading, you must wait for confirmation. If you are trading shares and are using a daily chart, wait for 2-3 days and see what happens. If you see confirmation then you can open your trade, depending on whether you are trading long or short.

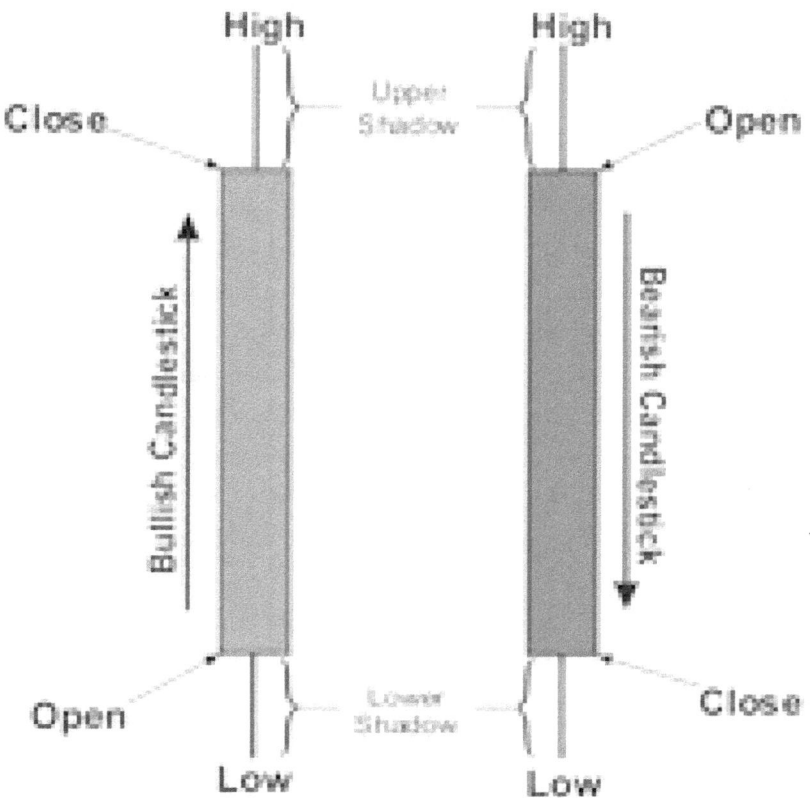

Finally, remember that candlestick analysis is an art not a science, and can be applied to any financial instrument in any time frame. It takes many months and years of practice to interpret them correctly, but once learnt they provide the most powerful analysis of future price movement available. Combine them with a western indicator such as volume, and you start to be able to read the market and correctly predict future price movements.

The Top 12 Candlestick Indicators

If you have been trading for more than two weeks, you probably know about candlesticks. They are one of the most innovative tools in enlightening a trader on day-to-day momentum. They are excellent for intraday trading and, more importantly, for entry and exit signals.

The other four tools-support/resistance, Fibonacci retracements, ATR, and MAs-can give you set numbers to target candlestick charts to seal the deal.

As I suggested in the macro technical analysis, you have to have some redundancy in your trading indicators to answer the core questions, "Where is the market going?," "How fast is it getting there?," and "When will it arrive?" You need the same type of redundancy in the micro analysis of entry and exit. Candlesticks do just that; once you have your favorite entry/exit price selection technique, use the candlesticks to set up the timing.

If you are unfamiliar with candlestick patterns, they employ two-dimensional bodies to depict the open-to-close trading range and upper and lower stems (or shadows) to mark the day's high and low. Steve Nison introduced the United States to candlestick charts, although they had been used in Japan since the sixteenth century.

While there are volumes of books and videos on the various types of candlestick patterns, we have only two goals when we use candlesticks: (1) we want it to confirm our entry or exit into or out of a trade, and (2) we want it to confirm a market's turnaround or continuation.

When we know the price at which we are entering or exiting the market, we want to give it a 2- to 4-day time period to let the proper candlestick pattern to show up to confirm our trade. Once we get the confirmation, we act immediately!

I have narrowed down the candlestick chart patterns to 10 key patterns that I watch. You can use my set, or you can use/develop your own set. Even with the 10 that we see here, you will find that you may favor just a few as confirmation indicators.

The trick to understanding how to apply candlesticks is to realize that they can give you information for only a limited time. They are not designed to be a macro indicator, but they are great at gauging the market's sentiment right now.

They do not necessarily give you a price to enter or exit; they just tell you the "when," which is important if you already have an opinion of the market, but if you do not have an opinion, you can find yourself chasing every candlestick pattern with little discretion, which can be detrimental in the long run. When you have an overall context on how you are approaching the market, the candlestick patterns are the icing on the cake.

Memorize these candlestick patterns. Photocopy these pages and make flash cards if need be-just remember them so that when you have all of the setups in place, you simply can see the proper candlestick and execute the trade.

There is some overlap between the various entry and exit technical analysis tools and the macro tools, particularly when it comes to answering the question, "When will the market arrive?" That's perfectly fine. We have taken a top-down approach to the technical analysis that will allow us to look at a chart and within a few minutes be able to determine how and when we will interact with the market.

Having exact prices to target is what is all important. Now that we have discovered the prices we are targeting for our entry and exit, we are capable of matching them up with the proper risk management technique that will help us have the optimum opportunity for success.

Top 12 Candlestick Indicators and What They Look Like

1. Doji: A doji line that gaps from a long green candlestick.

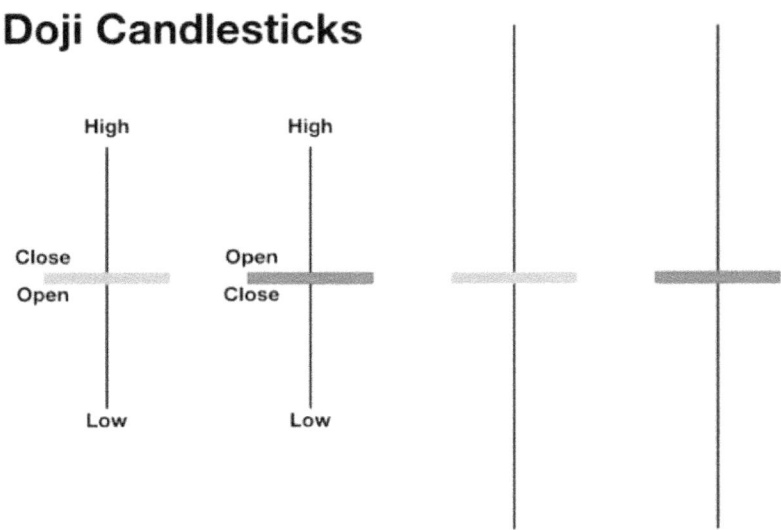

2. Bullish engulfing signal: A bullish engulfing pattern occurs when buying pressure overwhelms selling pressure, reflected by a long green real body engulfing a small red real body in a downtrend.

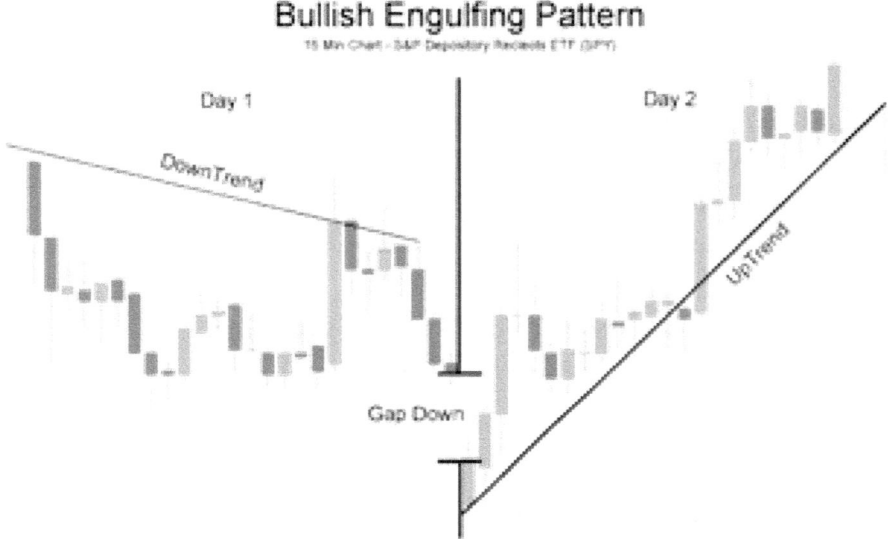

3. Bearish engulfing signal: A bearish engulfing pattern occurs when selling pressure overwhelms buying pressure, reflected by a long red real body engulfing a small green real body in an uptrend.

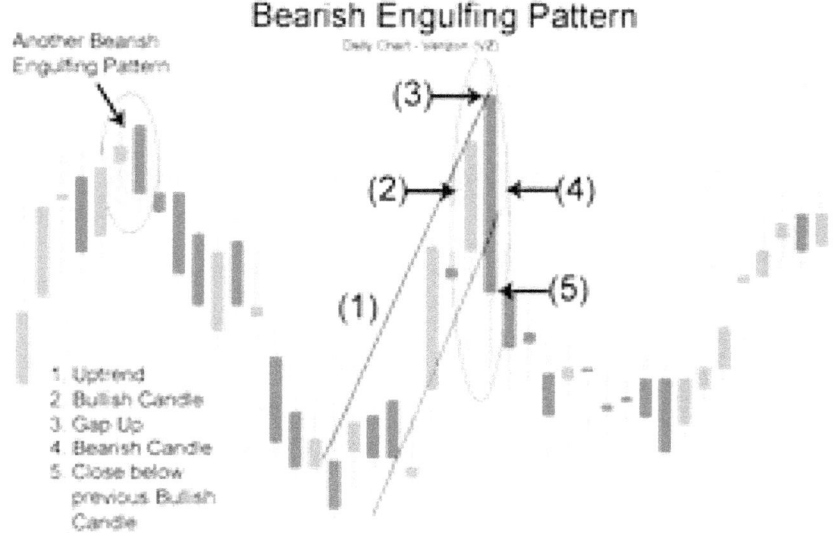

4. Hanging man: A small real body (green or red) with little or no upper shadow. It is a bearish reversal pattern when appearing during an uptrend.

5. Bearish shooting star: A candlestick with a long upper shadow with little or no lower shadow and a small real body near the lows of the session.

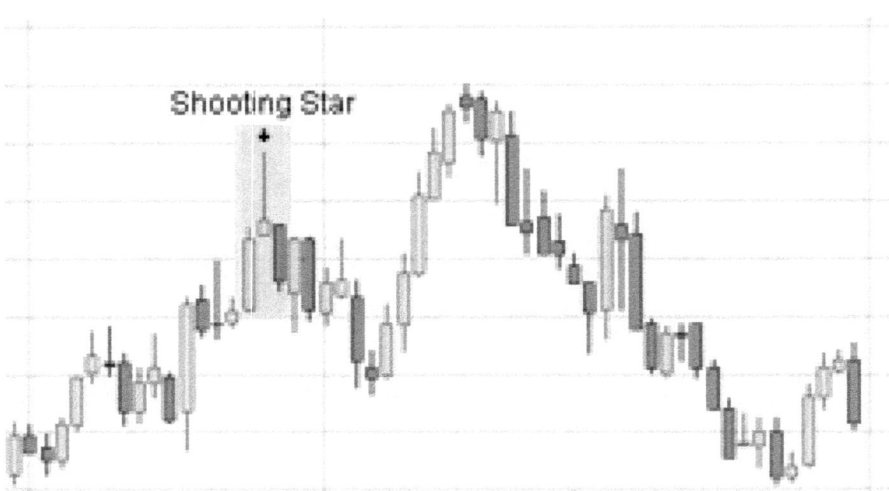

6. Bullish hammer: A bottoming candlestick line with a small real body (red or green) at the top of the trading range with a very long shadow with little or no upper shadow.

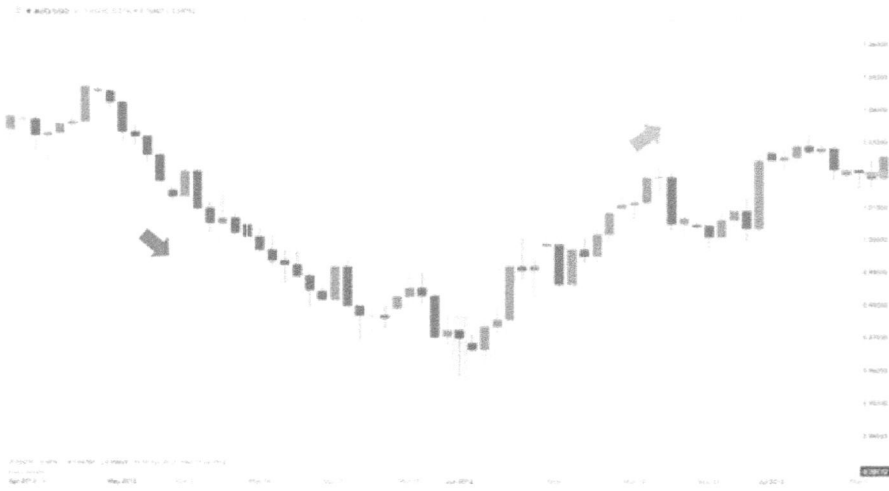

7. Inverted hammer: A candlestick that has a long upper shadow and a small real body at the lower end of the session. It is a bullish bottom reversal signal.

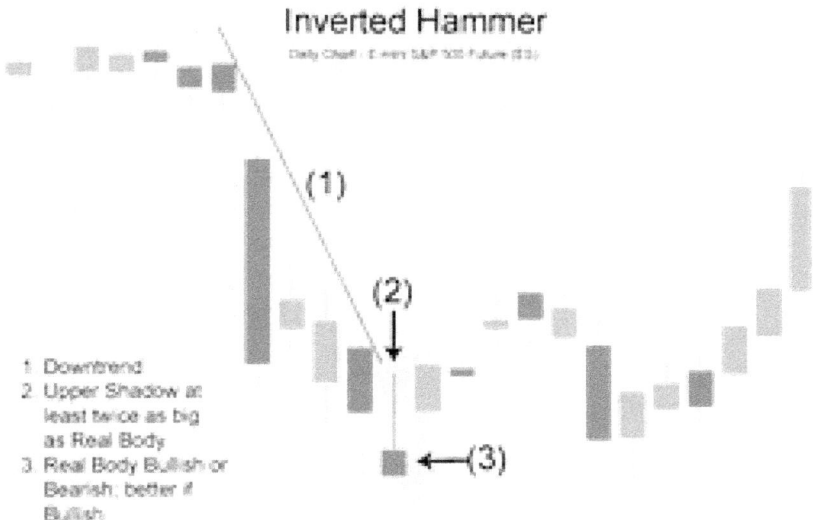

8. Bullish harami: A two-candlestick pattern in which a small real body holds within the prior session's unusually large real body. The harami implies that the preceding trend is getting ready to conclude.

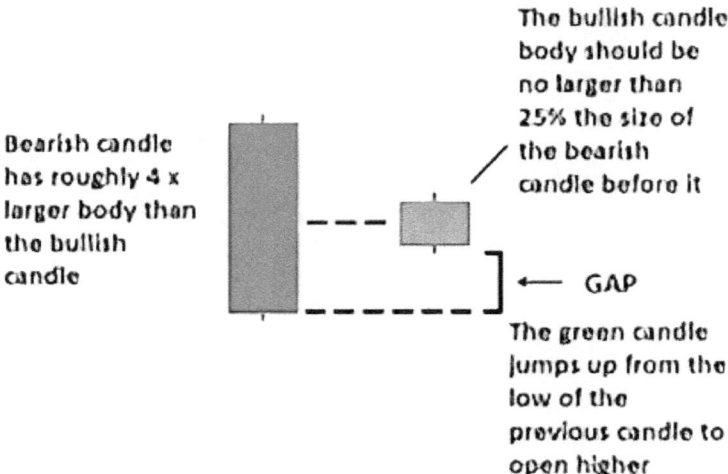

9. Bearish harami: A two-candlestick pattern in which a small real body holds within the prior session's unusually large real body. The harami implies that the preceding trend is getting ready to conclude.

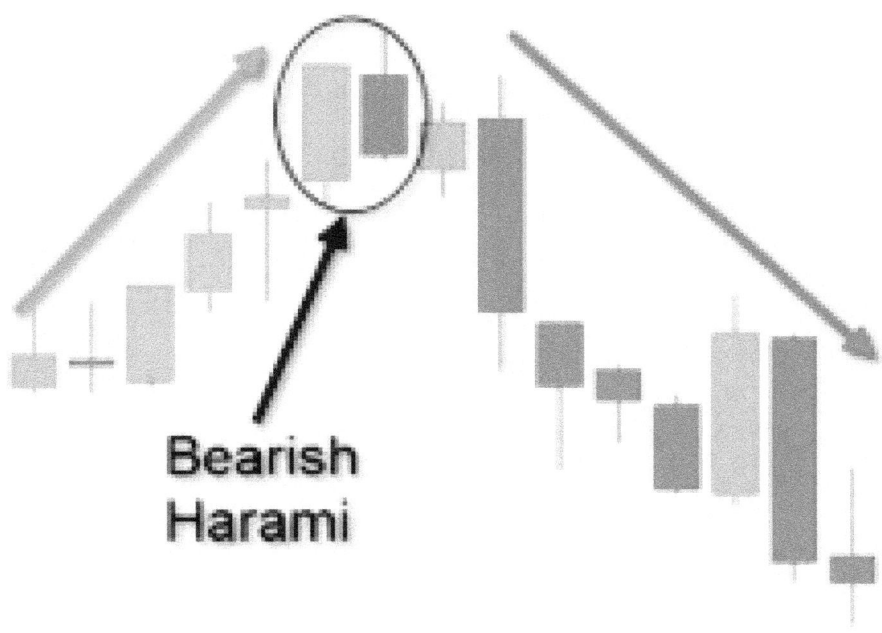

10. Dark cloud: A bearish reversal signal. In an uptrend, a long green candlestick is followed by a long red candlestick that opens above the prior green candlestick's high. The second candlestick must close well into the first candlestick's real body.

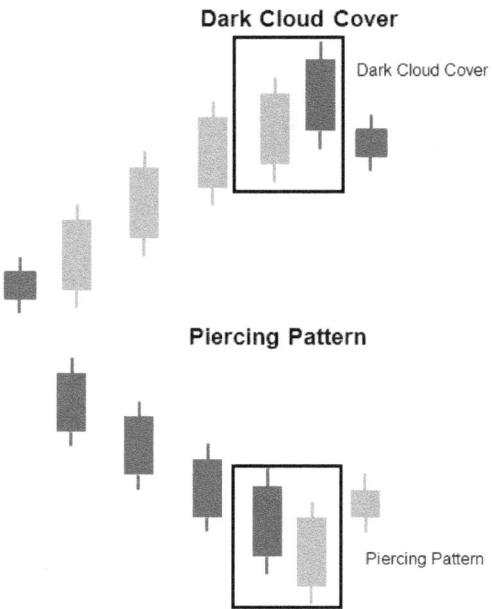

11. Piercing pattern: A long red candlestick is followed by a gap lower during the next session. This session finishes as a bullish green real body that closes more than halfway into the previous session's real body.

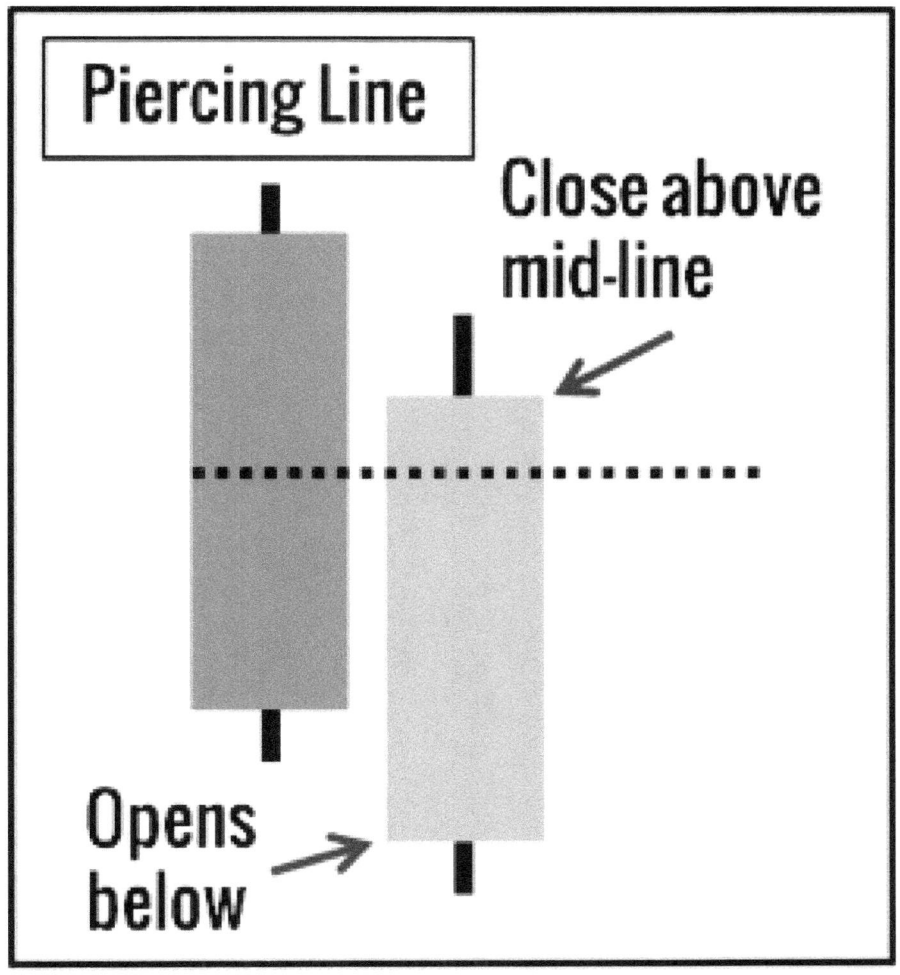

12. Bearish/bullish kicker signal: The first candle opens and moves in the direction of the trend, either up or down, depending on whether or not it's a bullish or bearish kicker signal. The second day's candle opens at the same price of the previous day and goes in the opposite direction. This means the two candlesticks must be opposite colors (one white and one black). It's important to remember that the candle of the second day should never retrace the previous days trading range.

Kickers

Bullish Kicker   Bearish Kicker

Chapter 6: Trend Following: Moving Averages

Historical Evidence

Moving averages are among the most popular and simplest methods of trading. Simply put, it is done by calculating the mathematical mean of a given set of values. In other words, a set of numbers - say the closing prices within a 10-day period – are added up together and divided by the number of values in that set.

The resulting number is the moving average, not just a regular average or mean due to the nature of trading. Since old data must be dropped from the set and new values must come and replace them, this value is dynamic as opposed to static. Once these points are plotted onto a chart, they are connected to create a moving average line.

Take a look at this simple moving average chart above. The blue line represents a moving average of 50 days. You will notice that the trend has been continuously moving lower since 2007, reaching its average in January 2008 as it begins to dip.

Defining Entry Points

Using the same chart, we can determine the entry point for this trading system. When the chart crosses below a moving average, it suggests that the asset price will likely continue to fall. This can be seen as a trade signal for entry for those traders who believe they can profit from a decline in stock prices. Conversely, when the price crosses above the moving average, the asset price may be ready to increase. This can also signal another entry point for the trader who purchases securities in order to sell them later at a higher price.

Defining Exit Points

Exit strategies typically involve setting up prior stop-loss limits to avoid the emotional response of being too confident that the trend will continue and missing out on other opportunities. A common exit strategy for moving averages is exiting on strength. The day trader will need to look for a signal of strength towards the direction of his first initial entry and make the exit. This way, the trader can lock in his profits before the rest of the market jump on the bandwagon, which may prompt a possible reversal. Some of the indicators you can use to determine exit points are pivot target, percentage ATR, and oscillator extremes. These advanced technical terms and strategies need to be studied separately in order to further understand when the best time to exit would be.

Setting up The System

Now, how does one determine which is the best market to trade in? By using a concept called relative strength, you will be able to identify which is the best at any given time. Take a look at the charts below:

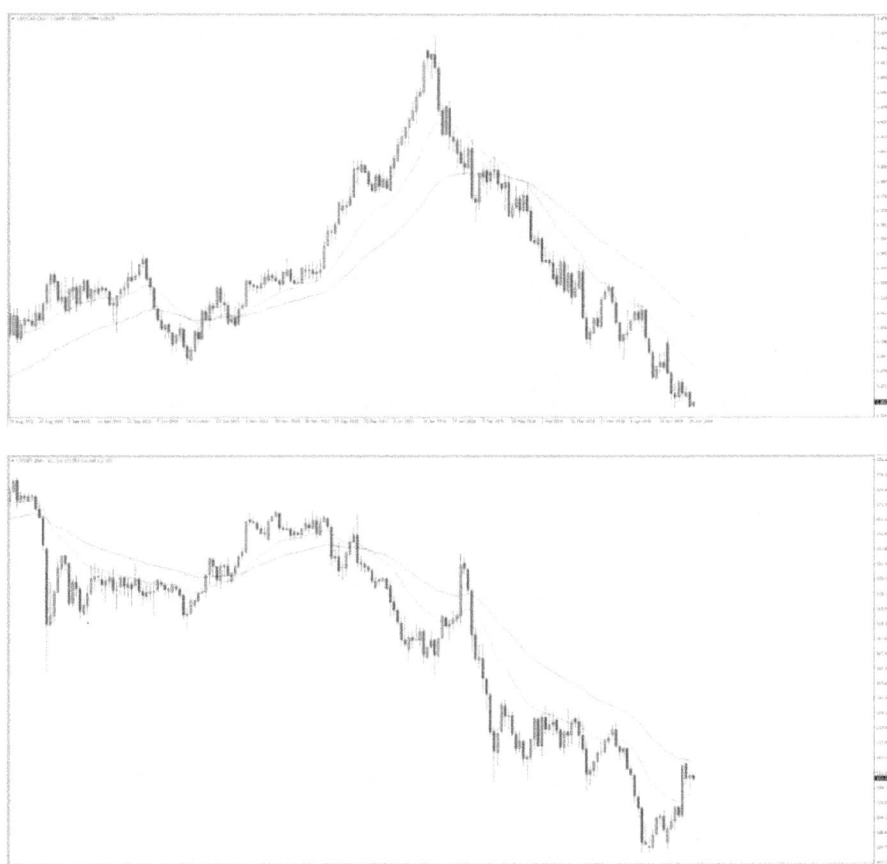

Compare the steepness of each chart's moving average. The steeper it is, the stronger/weaker the market will be. In this case, you would want to short the market in the first chart instead of the second chart where the market is relatively weaker.

Here is an example of how to use Moving Averages in trading:

- If the 200-day moving average is increasing exponentially and the price is above the line, then there is an uptrend.

- If you are using the 20-50 day period of moving averages, wait for the two-test dynamic support.

- If this price test is supported twice, make your entry on the third try.

- Place a stop loss of 2 ATR if long, or exit when you're wrong.

- If the price moves according to your favour, then take profits when the candle closes beyond 50 exponential moving averages.

Below is a sample on how to trade using this system:

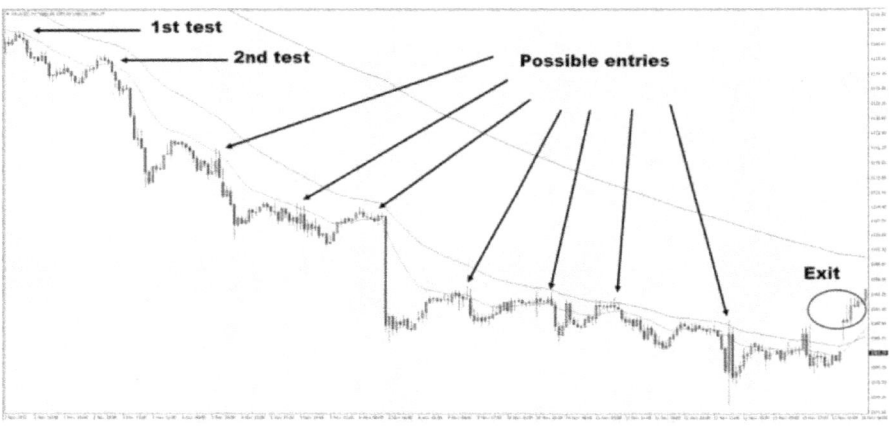

Chapter 7: Trend Following: Cross-Over of Moving Averages

Historical Evidence

Now that you know how moving averages work, understanding cross-over will be very easy. In a nutshell, it works in the same way as moving averages, but you will need to follow two lines instead of just one.

Defining Entry Points

This next figure uses two moving averages: short term (over a period of 15 days – red line) and long term (over a period of 50 days – blue line). This is the same as the first chart given above, but with the inclusion of 2 moving averages to determine entry strategy. When the two moving averages converge, it can be used as an entry point. You can also determine when a trend will about to end and reverse by simply plotting down a couple of moving averages on your chart and waiting for a crossover.

Defining Exit Points

What some traders do is that they make their exit once a new crossover has been made or once the price has moved against the position in a predetermined set of pips. Others will exit at a pre-determined stop-loss, because waiting too long may hurt your chances and be too late once a reversal becomes full blown.

Setting up the System

There are several ways to apply cross-over of moving averages, and two common ones are called the Golden Cross and the Silver Cross. In the Golden Cross method, you focus on 200 days of simple moving averages and 50 days simple moving averages. This strategy is widely accepted and more commonly used.

On the other hand, the Silver Cross uses 50 exponential moving averages above and 100 exponential moving averages. It was invented on the firm belief that exponential moving averages help to understand market conditions.

While cross-over moving averages work perfectly in a volatile and/or trending market, they don't do too well when the price is ranging. You will get hit with a number of multiple crossover signals and find yourself getting stopped out a lot of times before you get to catch a trend again.

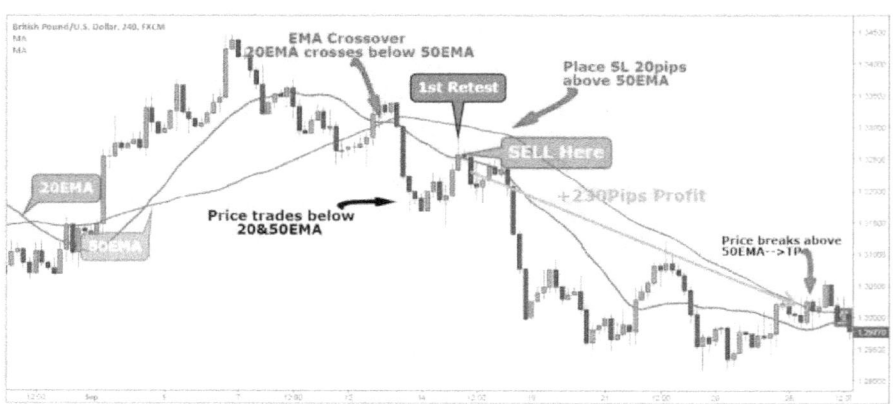

Chapter 8: Trend Following - Turtle Trading

Historical Evidence

In 1983, traders Richard Dennis and William Eckhart held the turtle experiment to show that anyone can be taught to trade. They found a group of people and by forking out money from their own pockets, allowed them to trade based on his instructions.

The idea of how turtle trading works lives by the principle of "the trend is your friend." This means buying futures when they are breaking out to the upside of trading ranges and sell short downside breakouts.

Defining Entry Points

In this chart, the entry point is established by buying on a new 40-day high. Here are the two ways these "turtles" entered the trade:

- Short-term system based on 20-day breakout

The Turtles entered when the price moved above the high of the last 20 days, or dropped below the low of the last 20 days. Trade was skipped if the prior signal was a winner, such as the price going 2N against the position, before triggering a 10-day profitable exit.

- Longer-term system based on 55-day breakout

The Turtles entered when the price moved above the high of the last 55 days, or dropped below the low of the last 55 days.

The Turtles also did something called pyramiding, which is taking a larger position as the price moves favourably. Once they were in the trade, turtles added one unit to their position each time the price moved ½ N in their favour.

Defining Exit Points

The turtles ended a trade on the breakout, and always did so before the close of the daily market. A breakout is identified when the price of an asset "breaks" trough the high or low of a certain number of days.

At the onset of making the entry, a stop loss is placed 2N below the entry price if long, and 2N above the entry price if short. This served to cut losses if things didn't move favourably after entry. Another exit method is called the Whipsaw, where exit points were being placed at 1/2N away from the entry point. If the price didn't hit the stop-loss point after entry, then the turtles used an N-based system to exit.

- For system 1, the exit was a 10 day low for long positions, and a 10 day high for short positions.

- For system 2, the time period was extended to 20 days for both long and short positions.

It takes a lot of discipline to wait for 10 or 20 day low to exit a position. But avoiding the urge to get out and sticking to the system is control over you.

Setting up the System

The Turtle Trading System was set up in the early 80's, and there have been a lot of questions raised on its sustainability in the market today. In 1970-1986, this system enjoyed returns of 216%, which was followed by a decline to 10.5% during 1986-2009. However, it did manage to do well from 2004-2016, with max returns of 40%. So while it may not be completely new, it's not entirely obsolete either.

Chapter 9: Counter-Trend Following - Williams %R

Historical Evidence

The Williams percentage (%R) is a technical indicator which was developed by Larry Williams. It is used to identify whether an asset is overbought or oversold in order to determine possible turning points. It is a single line fluctuating on a reverse scale.

The %R is calculated as follows:

%R = (Highest High – Close) / (Highest High – Lowest Low) X -100

Nowadays, manual calculations are no longer needed as we have software readily available to us to do the work. The Williams %R is available on most trading platforms such as MetaTrader and ThinkorSwim, as well as on free online charting sites such as Yahoo!Finance and StockCharts.com.

Defining Entry Points

Use a simple 18-day moving average of closing prices. Look for 2 consecutive lows in this 18-day moving average. Then, perform your entry when the price rallies above the higher of the two bars above the 18-day moving average.

Defining Exit Points

Place your stop loss for the trade below what your buying price or after an 18-bar sell signal.

Setting up The System

The main goal of the Williams Percentage R is to identify shares that were overbought or oversold, and can be an indicator within trend analysis. Here are some rules:

- If the indicator climbs above -20, the asset may be overbought.
- If the indicator drops below -80, it may be oversold.

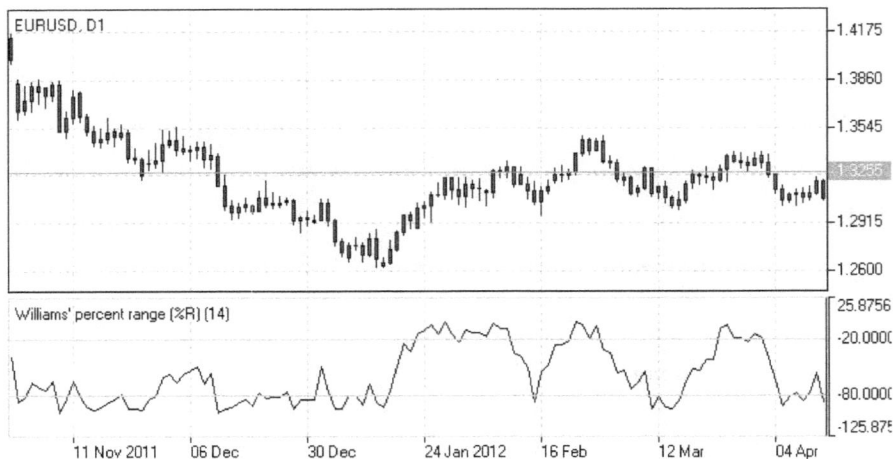

Looking at the extremes in this chart, the indicator may suggest possible turning points:

- Williams Percentage Range signals a possible sell opportunity by crossing the overbought boundary above.

- Williams Percentage Range signals a possible buy opportunity by crossing the overbought boundary below.

While divergence patterns are rare, it may indicate possible weakness:

- Uptrend weakness if the price climbs to a new high but the indicator does not

- Downtrend weakness if the price falls to a new low, but the indicator does not.

In a nutshell, the Williams Percentage R strategy can be summarised as follows:

- Buying when the market is oversold (%R reaches -80 or lower)

- Selling when the market is overbought (%R reaches -20% or higher)

Chapter 10: Counter-Trend Following - Relative Strength Index

Historical Evidence

The Relative Strength Index (RSI) is undoubtedly one of the most popular indicators in the market. It is basically a measure of how well a stock is performing against itself by comparing the rises and drops during the days. It has a range of 0 to 100; above 70 RSI is considered bullish, meaning the investors are optimistic of the rise in prices, while a reading below 30 is bearish, where the market is in decline and investors are attempting to take profit.

This method may result in several days before trading signals occur, but when they do, there's is a better winning percentage than some of the more active strategies. And since it doesn't need to involve trading every day, it can be used as a supplement to a more active method. This trade works best when trades are signalled in the direction of a long-term trend. When there is no prevailing trend, the signals can be taken in either direction. When the daily ADX is rising, the day trades should be done only in the direction of the trade, and when it is in decline, the trend can go either way.

Defining Entry Points

Entering the trade using the RSI Strategy is very straight forward. You wait for the price to head in the direction of the trade and wait for the first candle to close above the candle that was identified as the previous 50-low candle.

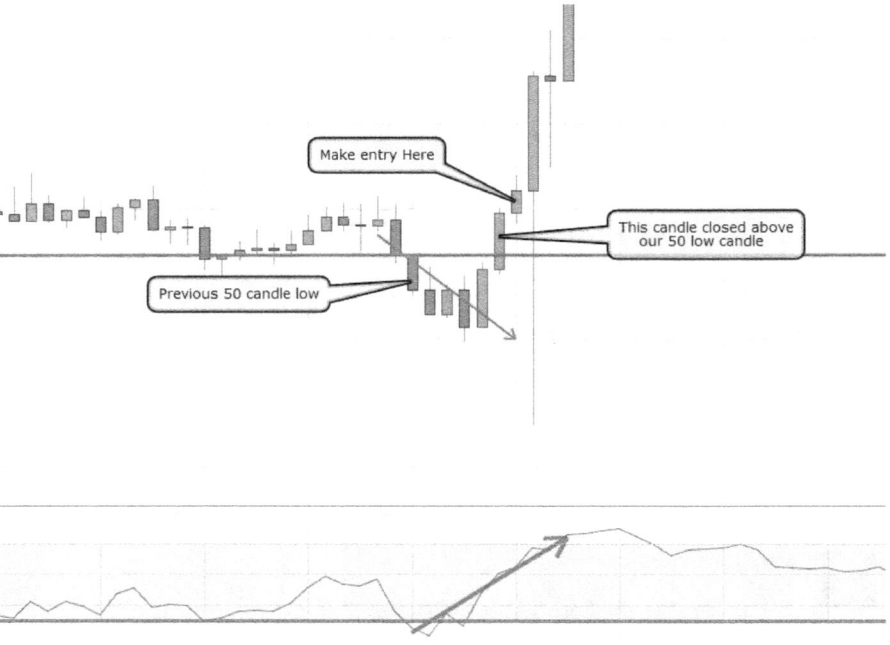

Defining Exit Points

As soon as you place your entry, place the stop loss. To place your stop, bump back 1-3 time periods and find a reasonable level to put your stop that makes logical sense.

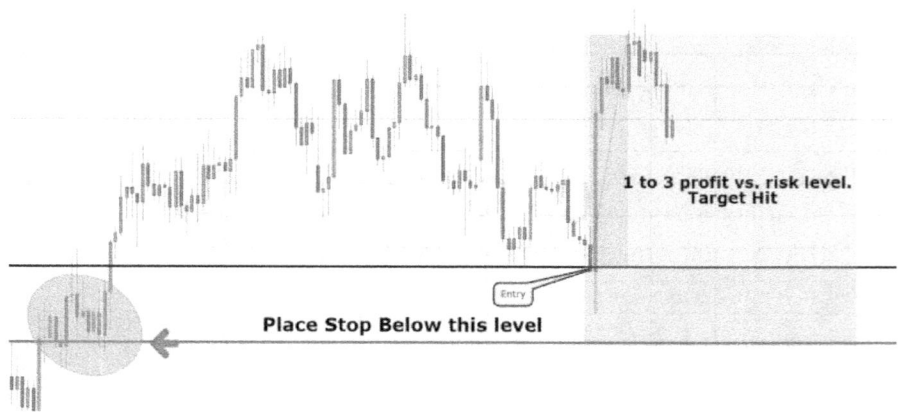

Follow at least a 1 to 3 profit vs. risk level. This will ensure that you are maximizing your potential to get the most out of this strategy.

Setting up The System

Here are several points in order to set up this system:

- Find the pair that is showing a high in the last 50 candlesticks. Or depending on the trade, identify the low.

- Once we find 50-candle low, we need it to be coupled with RSI reading of 20 or lower. If it's a high, it needs to be coupled with the RSI reading of 80 or higher.

- Wait for a second low price candle to close after the previously identified first one.

- Enter the trade by waiting for a candle to close above or below the first candle you have previously identified.

- Place a stop loss immediately after gaining entry.

Chapter 11: How Much Money Is Required To Start Day Trading?

Day trading today is so different then what it was back when I first started trading in 1989. In those days, most trading was done in what is called a Trading Pit, where securities and commodities were bought and sold via "open outcry."

Like in the movie "Trading Places" with Eddie Murphy and Dan Aykroyd, where you see all these people in different colored jackets shouting and waving their hands (called Floor Traders), surrounded by electronic price displays and news monitors.

When you wanted to make a trade, whether it be for a day trade or longer, you would pick up your telephone and call your broker, who would take your order over the phone and then, after confirming the order back to you, would relay it to someone else and eventually end up in the hands of one of these Floor Traders. The Floor Trader would then attempt to fill your order in the Trading Pit, and if filled, relay that information back to your Broker who would then call you back with your fill.

When it comes to Day Trading, where you need to get in and out of your trades quickly, the old way was not very efficient and at times frustrating and costly. A lot can happen in the time it takes for orders to arrive at the Pit and come back to you as a fill.

With the improvement in communication technology as the 20th Century was coming to a close, Electronic Trading (aka eTrading) became more prevalent and accessible to the every day trader. With just a click of your computer mouse, buy and sell orders could be placed instantaneously. If your price is met, you could be filled before your hand even moved away from your mouse.

Electronic Trading is arguably responsible for the major reduction in trading costs (commissions) seen over the years, as well as the increase in Day Trading activity. Not only can Day Traders make quick trades, but their cost per trade is also much lower than years before. Today, anyone with a small amount of disposable funds (never use money you need to live on) can get setup and start Day Trading.

So how much money is required to get started in Day Trading?

This is one of the most asked question by individuals looking to get into trading. It is also one of the most difficult questions to provide a black and white answer to.

The amount of money needed to start Day Trading really depends on several variables. What are you interested in trading? The (discount) Broker you decide to open an account with. The style of trading you wish to do.

Day Trading in the Stock Market is not really suited for beginners. Recent regulations require that you deposit at least $25,000 in cash or securities with your brokerage before you can day trade securities.

The Futures and Commodity markets offer Day Traders better access to day trade for a much smaller deposit. Depending on the brokerage, you can open a futures account for as little as $2,500, although many require at least $5,000 to $10,000. This is not the same as "margin", which is the minimum amount of capital you must have in your account in order to trade a particular a futures contract. The margin required depends on the market being traded and the current level of volatility. For example, to trade a single Live Cattle futures contract may require that you have an "Initial Margin" of $1,650 in order to initiate the trade, and it must not drop below $1,200 which would be your "Maintenance Margin".

In recent years, the FOREX (Foreign Exchange) currency trading has taken the trading world by storm. With access to free price data and trading platforms, lower minimum account balance requirements, no commissions (brokerages make their money via the ask/bid spread), and flexible trading unit sizes, it has proven to be one of the best options for anyone looking to get into Day Trading with less capital requirement.

With futures trading, just a few ticks can mean several hundred dollars (profit or loss) for most contracts traded. If you are just starting out and your account balance is only

$3,000 to $5,000 (or even $10,000, which is not that much in futures), you could be seeing moves of 10% of your account within minutes!

It is great when your timing is right and the market is moving in your favor. It is not so great when your timing is off by just a little and it is moving against you. For a Day Trader just starting out, it can be very difficult to succeed with this kind of leverage in futures with a small account.

In the FOREX markets, however, you only need to find a FOREX brokerage that gives you the flexibility of decreasing your unit size. While new regulations has tightened up the leverage available to traders (i.e. 250:1, 100:1), being able to adjust your unit size makes it possible for traders to trade pip sizes (think 'ticks') that are even less than $1 each. Some brokerages have "no minimum deposit" requirement to open an account.

Your only restriction for trading a currency pair is the amount you have on deposit in relation to the unit size you have chosen to trade, due to margin requirements. So if you have a small amount in your account (say just $200), simply adjust your unit trading size down so that you meet the margin requirement.

While a small pip size won't make you large profits during a single trading day, it also means you can avoid large losses as well. And if your day trading experience grows to where you are making consistent profits, those small gains can add up to increase your account size. With your account size increased, you can adjust your unit size up accordingly.

So if you are interested in getting started in day trading, if you choose to trade in the FOREX markets, you can do so for very little money.

Online Forex Day Trading The Tao Of Rapid Wealth Creation And Perpetuation

Foreign currency trading is the most profitable and powerful way to make money today in the world.

It is a 2.5 trillion dollars daily global market and business.

For this reason the knowledge and the secrets of how to do it successfully have been kept away from the public for thousands of years.

This is because it is the jealously guarded "SECRET" of how the "Money and Power" Elites, the multi-national and multi-billion dollars corporations, largest banks and governments of the world, the "Movers & Shakers" of International Banking & Finance, Business moguls & Tycoons, CEOs of major Corporations, secret societies and the privileged blue bloodlines of the Wealthiest Families of Europe and the Americas make their money and get rich.

They create vast fortunes easily trading foreign currencies.

Thereafter, using this great wealth, they create factories to manufacture consumer goods and products and hire you, Joe Bloke to work in those factories, banks and jobs at minimum wages.

So, it is no wonder why they don't want you to know about the real truth and "secret" on how to generate great wealth through foreign currency trading.

If you know how to trade foreign currency and generate $100,000 monthly for life, will you be idiotic, naïve and crazy to go to work at these DEAD END jobs to earn minimum wages and be paid nickels and dimes?

So, there has been a persistent organized campaign by the powers that be, the Money Elite to keep away and hide these "secrets" of creating vast wealth from foreign currency trading.

That is why they are always floating false propaganda and negative campaign in the mass media that currency trading is risky and you should not do it because you'll lose all your money.

If you go to your bank manager or money management advisor or investment management company and tell them that you wish to make money at home from online currency trading, they will scream at you and try to discourage you and frighten you with the false information and half truth that it is risky and that you'll lose your money.

This is because it is THE secret with which they make money and get rich!

Citibank alone makes $20 billion dollars trading currencies yearly.

Most banks, including your bank trade currencies and it is among the major ways to create income.

It is just that they don't advertise this secret.

George Soros, the King of Forex trading makes billions of dollars yearly trading currencies!

It is reported that a few years ago, he nearly caused the government of Thailand to go bankrupt because he made so much money trading their currency!

Yes, foreign currency exchange trading or Forex trading can be risky.

It is true, you can lose your shirt and go bankrupt.

But this is half of the truth.

The other half of the truth is that if you buy and study a good Forex currency trading e-book guide or program and understand how it works, avoid the pitfalls and get to know the secrets of risk management and trade with discipline, you can get fabulously rich so fast it will make your head spin round and put the devil to shame.

This is why there is an organized campaign to discredit online currency trading.

If you get rich so fast, then you'll not need to depend on the "Money and Power" Elites and their jobs and welfare system where they allow you nickels and dimes to keep you subjugated.

If you get rich too fast, they will no longer be able to manipulate you into voting and keeping them in power to continue milking your life by making you labor and work yourself to death making them rich.

There are so many reasons why most beginners in foreign currency trading fail to earn money and instead lose all their savings.

When they first hear about how easy and fast it is making money from day trading currency, they search the internet and find a Forex trading broker.

Then they open a currency trading account and put in a few thousands of dollars in the online currency trading account and immediately begin to try to earn money from online currency trading.

And they get entangled in all the foreign currency trading sophisticated strategies and systems of technical and fundamental analysis such as reading "Forex charts," "Moving Averages," "Elliot wave," "Stochastics," "Bollinger bands," "Directional movement index," "Trend and Oscillator indicators," "Fibonacci retracements and others.

They spend all day and night listening to business news on radio, reading Forex newsletters, Forex articles in magazines and watching business news on TV.

These beginners don't take their time to buy a valid online currency trading e-book guide to study and understand the Forex market and the currency trading "SECRETS" before they begin trading.

They don't open the free demo trial Forex trading account to practice for free to develop viable profitable currency trading skills first before they open a paid Forex trading account to begin trading and making real money.

They make the fatal and dumb mistake of trying to fly in the world of foreign currency trading market before they learn how to crawl.

So, they get confused, make grievous foreign currencies trading errors and lose their money.

When they lose their money, they will not accept responsibility because that is the difficult part.

The easy thing to do is to blame their mistakes on online currency trading and to declare and gripe that it is risky and a scam designed to con the unsuspecting public.

This gives them the justification to begin filing false complaints and instigating legal action with the lame excuse that they were naïve and didn't know the risk involved and so have been ripped off.

The truth is that there are at least one million people around the world who have foreign currency trading skills and do it well to make millions of dollars monthly!

Yes, sometimes they will lose.

But most of the time they are fabulously profitable.

I once read about a taxi cab driver from New York who started trading foreign currencies about 10 yrs ago.

While driving his taxi cab, occasionally during his lunch break, he will log into his Forex trading account and enter a few currency trades.

By the end of his driving day shift, he would check his online currency trading account and was always surprised to find that for a few minutes of trading currencies, he had made more money that day in minutes than he made driving the cab for a whole month.

This encouraged him to stop driving the taxi cab and to begin trading currencies full time.

In 10 years, he made $4 billion dollars ($4,000,000,000) trading foreign currencies online and was listed in Forbes Magazine's 400 richest Americans!

He is just one out of the many average people all over the world who took the time to study online currency trading, understood it and trade it correctly and are making millions of dollars without any hard work.

You too can do the same.

It is simple.

If you can click your mouse once to buy the currency and in a few minutes click your mouse a second time to sell them, you can make money.

It is a no brainer. Even a caveman can do it!

So, foreign currency trading is not difficult to understand or to do like stock or bond or commodity trading.

If you know where to get a good and valid Forex trading guide or e-book and be patient to spend 1 hr daily to study it to understand the foreign currency trading market, how to click your mouse to buy and sell the currency; and if you will be patient to do the free demo trial for a few months before you open a paid Forex trading account to begin trading, you can get obscenely and insanely rich so fast, it will make your eyes want to pop out, seeing all the piles of cash you generate just by clicking your mouse twice for a few minutes daily!

One powerful secret that will help you as a beginner is to avoid hiring money managers at the beginning to trade currencies for you.

The reason is that 90% of these money managers who advertise with highly impressive websites and brochures and also in TV infomercials and radios and seminars are fraudulent.

When you hire them to trade for you, they will over trade your account (churning) so as to generate a lot of trading fees for themselves because whether they make money for you or not, you must pay them their fees.

The more they trade your account, the more fees they generate for themselves!

By over trading your Forex currency account, they expose it to massive risk which will eventually lead you to lose a lot of money.

This is because there are certain days and times which are profitable to trade and there are some days and times which are not.

Therefore by over trading (churning) your currency trading account, they get rich at your expense.

Plus, some of them will even use some profits they generated from trading your account to trade for themselves and make themselves rich without you knowing what is going on.

As if that is not bad enough, some will entice you to trade on margin. This means that they will loan you money to trade.

But the trick is that they are loaning you digital money which is created from the air and has no value.

All they do is go to your account and enter any amount of money they wish to loan you. (They don't actually put real money into your currency trading account!)

This is not real money because it is just digital artificial numbers.

But if you use this fake funny digital money to trade and lose, then you'll owe them real money!

You'll be required to pay them with real money!

And if you fail to pay them, they can freeze your bank accounts, assets and homes to collect the debt.

This is how most of these brokers get rich at the expense of naïve beginners in online foreign currency trading.

So, if you're a beginner, avoid hiring money managers to trade for you at the beginning. Stay away from managed trading.

Instead learn to trade and after you have made at least $500,000, contact us to give you the list of the best and honest money managers in the world (as well as the best forecasting services) who can trade for you and make you richer.

There is another fraud which some money managers perpetrate.

After you open a paid online currency trading account and put in thousands of dollars in there for them to trade for you, they use your money to trade for themselves.

Then they use a computer software to generate a fake Forex trading account statement for your Forex trading account which will show that you've lost money.

There is no way most people will find out, because you can't access their trading activities.

And sometimes even when you find a honest and reputable money manager to trade for you, when your account becomes profitable and you request to withdraw some of the money, they will begin to give you a run around, excuses and try to discourage you from withdrawing the money.

If you persist, you'll find out that suddenly your account will begin to lose money because they have softwares to manipulate it and generate dubious account statements to make it seem as if you've been losing money!

Above all, most beginners in Forex currency trading fail to earn money because they spend too much time in doing complicated Forex mathematics, reading charts, listening to business news on radio, TV and reading too many Forex newsletters and magazine articles, which are conflicting, confusing, time consuming and counter productive.

They spend so much time over stuffing themselves with Forex trading news and information that they become constipated with information and overwhelmed and so have little or no time to actually click their mouse to buy and sell the currencies and make money.

Most beginners also are unable to find and use a good currency trading system and software.

Some of them are even conned into buying outrageously expensive trading softwares and system for $4,000 from some companies who advertise on TV infomercials late at nights.

They don't know that they can get the same Forex trading system and softwares for free online at the websites of some Forex trading companies!

These $4,000 softwares are not for beginners and when we checked them out, we found they are complicated and not easy to use.

Infact after you manage to master how to use it, they will not help you to make more money!

So, it is not wise squandering your hard earned $4,000 to buy them.

If these over priced worthless Forex trading softwares work as they are advertised in seminars and infomercial, the companies will not be selling them.

Instead they will keep them secret and use them to make billions of dollars.

If you wake up tomorrow and discover you have a goldmine underneath your house, will you go out and advertise in TV infomercials and radios and seminars to sell your house for $4,000???

The truth is that most of these infomercial advertising Forex companies don't really trade currencies. They are just sales people. Shysters. Tricksters.

They make their money by peddling worthless Forex trading softwares to the naïve beginners for $4,000.

When you check one of these companies out (one of them has the audacity to call their worthless software "Forex Made Easy"), you'll discover that the CEO of this company actually admitted that not only that he does NOT use his $4,000 software to trade but he knows nothing about trading currencies!

He only lends his name to his company to use to market their worthless foreign currency trading software.

The company's pitchman who conducts the seminar is a sales man and he also doesn't trade currencies because he had committed fraud in the past and was barred from trading commodities.

While the CEO of the company runs infomercial and seminars peddling worthless Forex trading software for $4,000, he doesn't use it and doesn't trade currencies.

Instead he hired a money manager who trades the currencies for him!

So, if you're a beginner who desires to get rich fast from currency trading, you must know these insiders' "SECRETS" of currency trading market and the pitfalls and how to avoid all the fraudulent companies peddling worthless Forex trading e-books, books, softwares, systems and complicated trading strategies.

There are millions of them.

Beware because they are smooth operators who are very skilled in salesmanship and who can easily dazzle you with their big refined nonsensical English and so con you.

There are billions of dollars to be made in foreign currency trading and you can get abundantly rich trading these currencies online from home or office starting small.

But you must locate and buy a valid foreign currency trading e-book guide.

You must study it and understand it.

You must try the free demo account trading and do well in it before you can open a paid Forex trading account to actually begin making real money.

You must begin by trading only one or two currencies at the beginning.

With time as you acquire more skills, you may trade more currencies.

You must learn how to trade with discipline and learn the BEST DAYS AND HRS to trade to be profitable and the other times when YOU MUST NOT TRADE to avoid losing money.

You must know how to "go long" or "short" on a currency, how to enter "Market Order," "Limit Order," "Stop Order," "OCO order" and "Entry Order."

If you learn how to do Online currency trading hedging, it will help you to maximize your profits.

You must be disciplined and avoid emotional currency trading.

When you make a reasonable amount of money for the day, stop trading because you can't be profitable at all times of the day and if you don't stop and take your profit, you may end up losing all the money you made.

Above all don't open a paid currency day trading account and trade until you have done the free trial demo account trading for a few months and mastered it.

At the beginning, keep your trading strategies simple.

Avoid complications and advanced trading strategies of technical and fundamental analysis because these are the reasons why 90% of beginners lose money.

Use a simple trading strategy to get rich at the beginning.

Afterwards you may then take advanced Forex trading courses and do technical, fundamental analysis and use forecasting services to make even more profits and get richer, making millions of dollars effortlessly.

If you're serious in learning all the insiders' "SECRETS" about how to make millions of dollars trading foreign currencies online, without selling your soul to the devil and without losing your shirt, you must get our powerful currency trading e-book which reveals a very simple and yet profitable and powerful trading strategy which is guaranteed to make you $100,000 monthly for life from home or office.

You can learn to get rich from the jealously guarded foreign currency trading "SECRETS" of the "Money and Power" Elites, the multi-national and multi-billion dollars corporations, largest banks and governments of the world, the "Movers & Shakers" of International Banking & Finance, Business moguls & Tycoons, CEOs of major Corporations, secret societies and the privileged blue bloodlines of the Wealthiest Families of Europe and the Americas.

With the millions of dollars which you make from foreign currency trading, you'll be free like a bird to buy a mansion, with the most lavish and expensive furnishings, jewelry, antiques, electronics, a 50ft yacht, dream luxury cars, pick your choice: Lexus X470, $44,000 Jaguar 2007 S type, Silver Porsche Carrera, $180,000 Ferrari Testarossa, Mercedes 2007 Model S Class, 2007 Rolls Royce Silver Seraph, Bentley Mulsanne S, $220,000 Bentley Arnage Silver Tempest or a flaming red Lamborghini Jalpa!

You can make all your dreams in life to come true, without any hard work!

May these insights into foreign currency online investing, foreign currency trading program, investing online, Forex trading, day trading, online trading e-book, day trading online, day trading system, day trading course, day trading future, Forex day trading, day trading book, day trading firm, day trading training, currency day trading, online future trading, online currency trading, online Forex trading, online commodity trading, online currency trading system, currency Forex online trading, online trading course, online trading education, trading, online trading investing, Forex, Forex trading, Forex broker, Forex market, Forex trading system, Forex news, Forex trader, Forex signal, Forex trading, online Forex, trade Forex, Forex quote, Forex education help you make millions of dollars and to achieve your life's ambitions and dreams.

Chapter 12: The Secrets to Day Trading Success

While trading systems vary and can be used in a multitude of ways, having a proven, reliable strategy is one of the single most important factors in the success of day trading. But even when armed with the best strategies, you can still potentially lose a lot of money. And this has nothing to do with incompetence, luck, or the system itself. The art and science of day trading relies on experience, good money management, discipline, and guidance. By examining the pitfalls of trading, you will be able to identify why most traders fail, thus learning from these mistakes and knowing how to avoid them.

- *Learn to identify the direction of the market*

As an effective day trader, one should learn how to pinpoint when the market is going up or when it is going down. Take advantage of trendlines and educate yourself as much as you can. By properly predicting these trends, you will have a higher chance of being able to make a successful entry, and a profitable exit.

- *Don't be greedy*

While being in the trading industry makes it difficult not to be greedy, one should exercise a certain kind of self-control and discipline. Day trading isn't a quick-rich strategy – rather, it is built on consistent, small wins. Fortunes are built on the accumulation of the small wins and it takes experience, patience, and determination in order to get there eventually.

- *Always know when to exit*

Losses may be a part of day trading, but there should be a limit as to when you are giving away too much "room" for these shrinking values. Make it a point to ensure that your average loss should be always be smaller than your average win, because it's the only way to ensure you're still making small profits even if your winning percentage is only 50%.

- ***Avoid trading in the wrong markets***

Stay away from a market that is only moving sideways. Instead, trade on those that are moving either up or down. Refrain from focusing on only one kind of market or only on certain stocks.

- ***Solidify your trading strategy***

This cannot be stressed enough – having a solid trading strategy is the most important thing you need to work on in order to come to trading prepared, and well-informed. Without it, you are just basically gambling. Remember that trading involves risks, albeit calculated ones at that.

- ***Control your emotions***

Being greedy, fearful, panicky, indecisive, or too excited can take a toll on your trading style. In order to effectively implement your strategy, the best way is to just stay calm. Don't allow your emotions to take control over you.

- ***Don't Overtrade***

Many day traders think that the more they trade, the more chance they have in hitting the perfect trade that will allow them to gain higher profits. Most traders trade out of greed, and some out of revenge to get back the money they've lost. There are even those that will continue to trade out of sheer boredom just because the market isn't moving the way they want. Whatever their reasons might be, try not to follow suit. Make a trade, stick to it, and exit appropriately. Don't enter everything all at once.

Chapter 13: The Seven Fundamentals for Day Trading

To become a consistently profitable trader you need to follow these seven fundamental steps before entering into the world of trading. Some of them you should do before and after each and every single trade you make:

1. Education and simulated trading
2. Preparation
3. Hard work
4. Patience
5. Discipline
6. Mentorship and a community of traders
7. Reflection and review

Education and Simulated Trading

Now that you have read this book, you should be in a better position to make a decision on whether or not day trading is right for you. Day trading requires a certain mindset, as well as a discipline and a set of skills that not everyone possesses. Interestingly, most of the traders I know are also poker players. They enjoy speculation and the stimulation that comes from it. Although poker is a type of gambling, day trading is not.

Day trading is a science, a skill, and a career, and has nothing to do with gambling. It is the serious business of selling and buying stocks, at times in a matter of seconds. You should be able to make decisions fast, with no emotion or hesitation. Doing otherwise results in losing real money.

After you've made up your mind and decided that you want to start day trading, the next step is to get a proper education. This book equips you with the basic knowledge essential for day trading, but you still have a long way to go before you will be a consistently profitable trader. Can you be a mechanic by just reading a book?

Can you perform surgery after reading a book or taking First Aid 101? No. This book develops a foundation that you can build upon. This book introduces straightforward trading setups to simply show what day trading looks like. It is not meant by any means to be a stand-alone book. You are not a trader yet, not even close.

I encourage you to read more books and find online or in-person courses on day trading. New traders often search for the best traders on the Internet. They think that learning from the most experienced traders is the best way to learn. On the contrary, I think new traders should look for the best "teacher." There is a difference.

Sometimes the best trader has no personality, or poor people skills, while a consistently profitable, but not one of the top 10 traders, can emerge as a premier lecturer, communicator, and mentor. New traders need to find the best teacher. You don't need to learn from the best traders to become the best trader. Think about who some of the best professional sports coaches are. Often they were not superstar players. They knew the sport, but their passion was for teaching and developing players. The skills needed to become a great trader are different from those required to be an effective trading coach. Being a star trader requires superior pattern recognition and discipline.

On the other hand, effective trading coaches are often obsessed with finding better ways to teach, are patient, and communicate clearly and effectively in a simple and easy-to-understand language. They can explain their methodology coherently. Often great traders lack the monetary incentive to create the best training program.

Trading in a Simulator

You should never start your day trading career with real money. Sign up with one of the brokers that provides you with simulated accounts with real market data. Some brokers give you access to delayed market data, but don't use those. You need to make decisions real time. Most of the simulated data software is a paid service, so you need to save some money for that software. Many trading rooms and trading educators offer simulator accounts.

DAS Trader offers the best simulated accounts for $120 per month (at the time of writing). Check out their website (www.dastrader.com) or contact them at support@dastrader.com for more information. This completes my unpaid and unsolicited advertisement for them!

If you use it for six months, and trade only with simulated money, it will cost you just $720. This is the cost of a proper education. If you are seriously considering day trading as a career, it's a small expenditure compared to the cost of an education for a new profession. For example, imagine that you want to go to school to get an MBA - it will easily cost you over $50,000.

Likewise, many other diploma or post-graduation programs cost significantly more than the education required for day trading.

Once you have a simulated account, you will need to develop your strategy. Try the strategies that I have discussed in this book, and master one or two of them that fit with your personality, available time, and trading platform. There is no best strategy among them, just like there is no best automobile in the market. There might, however, be a best car for you. The VWAP, Support or Resistance, and the Opening Range Breakout Strategies are the easiest and my favorites.

You need to only master a few of them to always be profitable in the market. Keep your strategy simple. When you have a solid strategy that you've mastered, make sure there is no emotion attached to it. Keep practicing it, and then start practicing a second strategy, and learn to incrementally add size in those strategies.

Practice with the amounts of money that you will be trading in real life. It is easy to buy a position worth $100,000 in a simulated account and watch it lose half of its value in a matter of seconds. But could you tolerate this loss in a real account? No. You will probably become an emotional trader and make a decision quickly, usually resulting in a major loss. Always trade in the simulator with the size and position that you will be using in the real account.

Otherwise, there is no point in trading in a simulated account. Move to a real account only after at least three months of training with a simulated account and then, start small, with real money. Trade small while you're learning or when you are feeling stressed. If you wish, you can always have a chat with me in our chatroom and receive some advice and guidance.

New traders often try to skip steps in the process, lose their money, and then give up their day trading career forever and tell themselves that it is impossible to make money by day trading. Remember, baby steps. Success in day trading is one foot forward and then the next. Master one topic, and then and only then move on to the next.

Most traders struggle when they first begin, and many do not have sufficient time in the morning to practice in real time. Those who can give trading more time when they start have a better chance to succeed. How long does it take to be a consistently profitable trader? I don't think anyone can become a consistently profitable trader in less than three or four months. After four

months of paper trading, you need at least another three months of trading in small share size to master your emotions and practice self-discipline and defensive money management while trading with real money. After six months, you may become a seasoned trader. Eight months is probably better than six months, and twelve months is perhaps better than both. Are you patient enough for this learning curve? Do you really want this career? Then you should be patient enough. Do you have this much time to learn the day trading profession?

It always amuses me when I see books or online courses and websites that offer trading education that will make a person money starting on day one! I wonder who would believe such advertisements.

You must define a sensible process oriented goal for yourself, such as: I want to learn how to day trade. I do not want to make a living out of it for now. Do not set an absolute income for yourself in day trading, not at least for the first two years. This is very important. Many traders think of inspiring goals such as making a million dollars or being able to trade for a living from a beach house in the Caribbean.

These goals may be motivating, and they definitely have their place, but they distract you from focusing on what you need to do today and tomorrow to become better. What you as a new trader can control is the process of trading: how to make and execute sound trading decisions. Your daily goal should be to trade well, not to make money. The normal uncertainty of the market will result in some days or weeks being in the red.

Often new traders email and ask me how they can become full-time traders while they are working at a different job from 9 a.m. to 5 p.m. New York time. I really don't have any answer for that. They probably cannot become a full-time trader if they cannot trade in a simulator real time between 9:30 and 11:30 a.m. New York time. You do not need to have the whole day available for trading, but you at least need the first two hours of market Open.

If you insist, I would say the first one hour of the market Open (9:30 to 10:30 a.m. New York time) is the absolute minimum time you should be available for trading and practice, in addition to any time you need for preparation before the market opens at 9:30 a.m. New York time. Sometimes I am done with trading and hit my daily goal by 9:45 a.m., but sometimes I need to watch the market longer to find trading opportunities. Do you have this flexibility in your work-life schedule?

When I started day trading, I was unemployed. Then I had to find a job to pay the bills because I was losing my savings on day trading. I am lucky I live in Vancouver (in the Pacific time zone) because I could trade and practice between 6:30 and 8:30 a.m. and then be at work for 9 a.m. Pacific time. If you don't have this luxury, maybe swing trading is better for you. But making a living out of swing trading is more difficult.

The best swing traders can expect an annual return of 20% on their account size. Day traders, on the other hand, look to profit between 0.5-1% of their account size daily. The currency market (Forex) is open 24 hours/5 days per week, and perhaps you could consider trading currencies and commodities if you do not have sufficient free time to practice day trading or swing trading. This book though is not a useful guide for swing trading or for the Forex market. They are both different from day trading in so many ways.

You must always be continuing your education and reflecting upon your trading strategy. Never stop learning about the stock market. The market is a dynamic environment and it's constantly changing. Day trading is different than it was ten years ago, and it will be different in another ten years. So keep reading and discussing your progress and performance with your mentors and other traders. Always think ahead and maintain a progressive and winning attitude.

Learn as much as you can, but keep a degree of healthy skepticism about everything, including this book. Ask questions, and do not accept experts at their word. Consistently profitable traders constantly evaluate their trading system. They make adjustments every month, every day, and even intraday. Every day is new. It is about developing trading skills, discipline, and controlling emotions, and then making adjustments continually. That is How to Day Trade for a Living.

Consistently profitable traders try to learn the process of trading and make good and fundamentally correct trades without thinking about the money. This is, of course, the opposite of amateurs, who are obsessed with making money every single day. Such thinking is your worst enemy. I am not trying to make money as a trader. My focus is on "doing the right thing."

All I am looking for is excellent risk/reward opportunities. And then I trade them. Being good at trading requires mastering the process of trading and the fundamentals of a good trade. Money is just the by-product of executing fundamentally solid trades.

As a new trader, you will be constantly looking at your profit and loss (P&L). P&L is the most emotionally distracting column in my trading platform. Plus $250, negative $475, plus $1,100. I tend to make irrational decisions by looking at it. I used to panic and sell my position when my P&L became negative although my trade was still valid according to my plan. Or, quite often, I became greedy and sold my winning position too early while my profit target had yet to be reached according to my plan. I did myself a favor and I hid my P&L column. I trade based on technical levels and the plan I make. I don't look at how much I am up or down in real time.

I'll note again, your P&L is not important when you first begin trading with real money, especially when you trade in smaller share sizes. On most trading platforms, there is an option to hide your real time P&L. If yours doesn't have it, then go old school and use some dark masking tape.

I say this seriously. I encourage you to go and find some masking tape and slap it on your screen. Your goal is to develop trading skills and not to make money. You have to focus on getting better every single day, one trade after another. That is How to Day Trade for a Living. Push your comfort zone to find greater success.

Preparation

John Wooden (or as some call him, the Wizard of Westwood), the famous American basketball player and coach, once said, "By failing to prepare, you are preparing to fail." Indeed.

There are two aspects to the preparation process for day traders:

1) the preparation necessary before the market opens (usually the night before or between 8 and 9:30 a.m. New York time), and

2) the specific trading information you must obtain before you can make a trade.

Wake up on time and get behind your PC early.

Review your scanners and shortlist your choices of stocks for the day. Review www.finviz.com or www.briefing.com and read about the fundamental catalysts that caused the stock to gap up or down. Compile information such as daily volume, intraday range, and short interest. Review daily charts and identify important levels of support or resistance. I do not make a trade unless I know the average volume, Average True Range, important technical levels, short interest, and fresh news for the Stocks in Play.

Shortlist your watchlist down to two or three stocks. During earnings season, there are many Stocks in Play to choose from. Each day, traders shouldn't choose more than two or three of these stocks to focus on. You can make considerably more money trading one or two stocks well instead of watching and trading many stocks poorly.

The earlier you start your morning the more time you will have to go through the news and find the best Stocks in Play. Sometimes in those extra minutes you find the stock of the day that you wouldn't have if you had spent less time researching. Moreover, you have extra time to ask members of your community about their choices of stocks and obtain their feedback. Most professional traders do not arrive later than 7:30 a.m. New York time.

Certainly experienced traders with a strong community and powerful scanners can stroll in later, but 9 a.m. is the latest that most serious traders arrive. Prepare physically. Drink enough water to hydrate during the morning stretch and do not become over caffeinated.

Being present in the pre-market is important. Every once in a while there will be an opportunity during pre-market trading to make quick money on a breaking news story. In addition, valuable information can be obtained by watching how stocks are being traded in the pre-market. Monitor the ranges of the stocks that are on your watchlist, identify intraday support or resistance levels, and confirm how much volume is being traded.

Often new traders will think that trading strategies can be reduced to a few rules that they must follow to be profitable: always do this or always do that. Wrong. Trading isn't about "always" at all; it is about each single trade, and each situation. Every trade is a new puzzle that you must solve. There is no universal answer to all of the puzzles in the market.

Therefore, you need to make a plan for each trade as early as when you are doing your pre-market scanning. Before making a trade, you must create a plan for your trades or a series of "if-then" statements. Develop some plans as to when you might take a position in one of your stocks on your watchlist. If you see the x scenario, then you will buy at this price. Continue creating "if-then" scenarios for each outcome.

For an example, let's take a look at Figures below Imagine you plan to trade DICK'S Sporting Goods, Inc. (ticker: DKS) on March 7, 2017. The stock had gapped down because of disappointing earnings reports and was being traded at around $50.50 at the pre-market. You think it might be a Stock in Play.

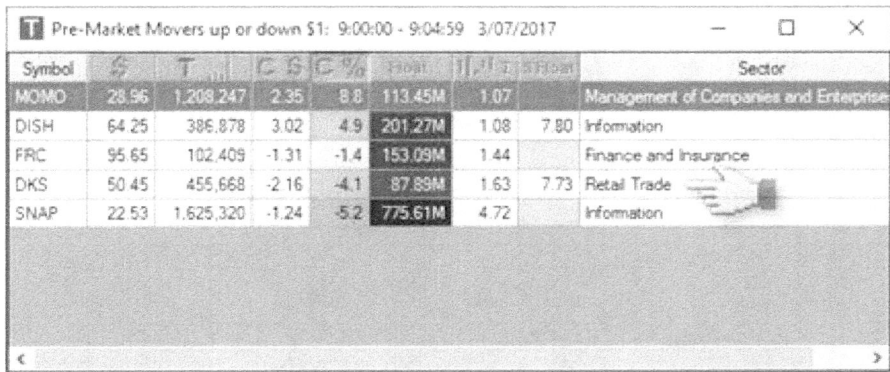

My watchlist at 6 a.m. (9 a.m. New York time) on March 7, 2017 - DKS is on my watchlist

Consider the different ways the stocks you have picked might trade and develop a series of if-then scenarios such as I've marked on Figure below:

Pre-market 5-minute chart of DKS on March 7, 2017 with my if-then statements noted. Market will open at 9:30 a.m. New York time.

If the price cannot push higher than VWAP in the first fifteen minutes of the market Open, then I will go short until the previous day close of $48.10.

If the price does sell off to the previous day close of $48.10, then I will go long and ride the reversal to the VWAP.

If the price pushes over VWAP with high volume, then I will go long and ride the momentum to sell at the next resistance level of $53.25.

If the price breaks over the daily level of $53.25, then I will go long again until the daily level of $55.50 (which is not shown on the above Figure 9.2).

On the other hand, if the price goes to $53.25, and that level acts as a strong resistance, then I will go short with the stock until it goes back down to VWAP.

You can write down your statements at the beginning of your trading career to make sure you stick to them, but after a few months of simulated trading you will learn how to quickly develop and review these statements in your mind. That is one of the most important outcomes of trading in a simulator: to practice and master if-then scenarios for your strategies and to process that information quickly. That is why three to six months of live simulated trading is essential as you begin your day trading career. As intraday traders, we develop theories daily.

In case you are wondering about DKS in the above example, it actually opened weak (below VWAP) and it was a good short trade toward the previous day close of $48.10 as you can see in Figure below. I then caught a smaller bounce from the previous day close to the VWAP with a long position.

5-minute chart on March 7, 2017 and my profit for that day (I also traded MEET, MOMO and MYL but they are not shown here and are not relevant to this example)

Hard Work

Hard work in day trading is different from what you might originally assume. A trader should not work 120 hours a week like investment bankers or corporate lawyers or other highly paid professionals do because, for us day traders, there are no end of the year bonuses. More than anything else, day trading is perhaps most similar to being a professional athlete because it is judged by one's daily performance.

Having said that, day traders should work hard, consistently and productively, each and every day. Watching your trading screens intently and gathering important market information is how we define hard work in day trading. You must ask the following questions constantly and at a rapid pace for several hours every day:

Who is in control of the price: the buyers or the sellers? What technical levels are most important?

Is this stock stronger or weaker than the market?

Where is most of the volume being traded? At the VWAP? Or the first five minutes? Or near moving averages?

How much volume at a price causes the stock to move up or down?

What is the bid-ask spread? Is it tradeable?

How quickly does the stock move? Is it being traded smoothly or is it choppy, jumping up and down with every trade?

Is the stock trading in a particular pattern on a 5-minute chart? How is the stock being traded on a 1-minute chart?

These are some of the questions that I ask myself and then answer before trading a stock. All of this information should be gathered before you make any trade. This is what we mean by hard work. As you can see, day trading is an intense intellectual pursuit which requires hard work. Remember Rule 2?

In addition, showing up every day to trade matters, either in your real account or in a simulator. If you search for support and resistance levels every day, including before the market opens, it will positively impact your trading in the long term. Turning off the PC early because a few trades went against you should be saved for special occasions when you really must clear your head.

Professionals often mentally recover after a few bad losses by switching to a simulator. I always encourage new traders in the simulator to continue trading until the Close and to find good opportunities to practice, especially since traders in the simulator are not under the same emotional stress as traders trading their own real money are. Of course, that does not mean that new traders should practice overtrading. Even when practicing in a simulator, with no commission and no real P&L, you should only trade sound strategies with excellent risk/reward opportunities.

I am often asked: "When you were in your first months of trading, did you ever feel like you couldn't do it?" The answer is YES, many times. I still, at least once a month, get really frustrated after a few bad losses and consider quitting day trading. Many times in my trading career I have wanted to quit and at times I have actually believed the myth that day trading is impossible. But I did not quit. I really desired to be a successful trader. I wanted the lifestyle and the freedom that comes with it. I paid the price for my mistakes, I focused on my education, and I eventually survived the very difficult learning curve of trading.

Patience

To become a consistently profitable trader, not only must you prepare properly and work hard, but you must also have patience.

Most successful trades are easy when you look at them after the fact, but finding them in real time is difficult and requires patience and hard work.

Watch, watch, and watch some more. If you are watching a stock, and it is not offering excellent risk/reward opportunities, then move on. Look at other stocks on your watchlist, and watch them intently. Consistently profitable traders spend trading days searching and watching for excellent risk/reward opportunities.

Successful traders are patient. They understand that they will not and should not be in every move. You should wait for opportunities with which you feel comfortable and confident. Professional traders realize that it is not enough to

buy a strong stock, or sell short a weak one. Entry price is extremely important. You have to open your positions at a price that offers the best risk/reward opportunity. Do not trade a strong stock that has moved away from a good risk/reward entry. That is called chasing the stock.

For example, if a stock is trading near a support and then breaks out downward, and you see a short selling opportunity but miss it, well, that is your first mistake. But if, out of frustration, you sell short that same stock well below that level, you have chased it. N ow you have made a bigger mistake. Chasing stocks is a deadly unforgivable sin in day trading. Missing the opportunity will not lose you any money (just an opportunity cost), but chasing the stock will. Do not let one mistake cause you to lose money with another one.

Discipline

Success in trading comes with skill development and self-discipline. Trading principles are easy, and day trading strategies are very simple. I have a Ph.D. in chemical engineering and I have worked as a research scientist at a world class facility. I have published numerous scholarly publications in high impact and respected scientific journals on my nanotechnology and complicated molecular level research. Believe me, I had to study and understand extremely more difficult concepts, so I can assure you that day trading, in theory at least, is easy.

What makes day trading, or any type of trading for that matter, difficult is the discipline and self-control that you need. You have no chance to make money as a trader without discipline, no matter your style, the time you commit to trading, the country you live in, or the market you are trading in.

Beginner traders who fail to make money in the markets often get frustrated and go out and try to learn more about how the markets work, study new strategies, adopt additional technical indicators, follow new traders, and join other chatrooms. They don't realize that the main cause of their failure is often their lack of self-discipline, their impulsive decisions and their sloppy risk and money management, not their technical knowledge.

Year after year, professional institutional traders perform so much better than private retail traders do. While most private traders are university-educated and thoughtful book-reading individuals who are often business owners or professionals, the average institutional traders are loud 20 something-year-old cowboys who used to play rugby in college and haven't read a book for many years.

Have you wondered why these guys outperform private traders year after year? It's not because they are younger or sharper or faster. They also don't win because of their training or platforms, since most of us retail traders have almost the same gear as they do. The answer is the strictly enforced discipline of trading firms.

Many successful institutional traders will quit their firm and go out on their own. They ask themselves, "Why should I share all of my profits with the firm, when I know how to trade and can keep all of the profit for myself?" Most of them lose money as private traders. They equip themselves with the same software and platforms, trade the same systems, and stay in touch with their contacts, but still fail. After a few months, most of them are back in a New York City recruiting office, looking for a trading job. How come those traders could make money for their firms but not for themselves?

The answer is self-discipline.

When institutional traders quit their firm, they leave behind their manager and all of the strictly enforced risk control rules. A trader who violates risk limits is fired immediately. Traders who leave institutions may know how to trade, but their discipline is often external, not internal. They quickly lose money without their managers because they have developed no self-discipline.

We private retail traders can break any rule and change our plan in the middle of a trade. We can average down to a losing position, we can constantly break the rules, and no one will notice. Managers in trading firms though are quick to get rid of impulsive people who break any trading rule for a second time.

This creates a serious discipline for institutional traders. Strict external discipline saves institutional traders from heavy losses and deadly sins (such as the averaging down of a losing position), which quite often will destroy many private accounts.

Discipline means you execute your plan and honor your stop loss as you set it out, without altering it in the middle of a trade. Discipline is executing your detailed plan every single time. If your plan is to buy a stock at VWAP and your stop loss is if it fails to hold

VWAP, then you must accept the loss immediately and get out of the trade if the stock fails to hold the VWAP.

Do not be stubborn about your decision if you are wrong. The market does not reward stubbornness. The market is not interested in how you wish stocks would trade. Traders must adapt to the market and do what the market demands. And that is the way day trading works and that is how it will always work.

There are going to be many days when you follow your plan, like in the above example, and then the stock will go back up and trade above VWAP after you were stopped out. In fact, there will be many times such as this in your trading career. But consider these two points: (1) Do not judge your trading strategy based upon one trade.

Executing your plan, and being disciplined, will lead to long-term success. Many times your plan will be fine and solid but a hedge fund manager out of nowhere will decide to liquidate a position in a stock that you are trading, the price will drop suddenly and you will get stopped out. You did not do anything wrong, it is the nature of the market that is unpredictable.

At times, the uncertainty of the market will leave you in the red. (2) A professional trader accepts the loss and gets out of the trade. You then re-evaluate and plan another if-then scenario. You can always get back into the stock. Commissions are cheap (for most of the brokers), and professionals often take several quick stabs at a trade before it will start running in their favor.

Trading teaches you a great deal about yourself, about your mental weaknesses and about your strengths. This alone ensures that trading is a valuable life experience.

Mentorship and a Community of Traders

Dr. Brett Steenbarger, the author of great books such as The Psychology of Trading and The Daily Trading Coach, once wrote:

"There is no question in my mind that, if I were to start trading full-time, knowing what I know now, I would either join a proprietary trading firm or would form my own "virtual trading group" by connecting online (and in real time) with a handful of like-minded traders."

You need to be part of a mastermind group that will add value to your trading career. T o whom can you turn to ask trading questions? I encourage you to join a community of traders. Trading alone is very difficult and can be emotionally overwhelming. It is very helpful to join a community of traders so that you can ask them questions, talk to them, learn new methods and strategies, get some hints and alerts about the stock market, and also make your own contributions. I

f you join me, you will see that I often lose money. It can be comforting to see that losing money is not limited to you, and everyone, including experienced traders, has to take a loss. As I've said, it's all part of the process.

There are many chatrooms that you can join on the Internet. Some of them are free, but most of them charge a fee. In our chatroom, you can see my trading platform and stock screener in real time while I am trading and listen as I explain my strategy and thought process. You can watch and listen. Or you can take your own trades, but still be part of our community.

It is extremely important to remember however, that if you are in any community of traders, either our chatroom at www.BearBullTraders.com or the dozens of others out there, you should not follow the pack or the room moderator, but you should be an independent thinker. Generally, people change when they join crowds. They become more unquestioning and impulsive, nervously searching for a leader whose trades they can mirror. They react with the crowd instead of using their minds.

Chatroom members may catch a few trends together, but they get killed when trends reverse. Never forget that successful traders are independent thinkers. Simply use your judgment to decide when to trade and when not to.

You need to find a trading mentor. A good mentor can positively impact your trading career in so many different ways. Today, because of algorithmic programs and market volatility, it's much harder for new traders to survive the learning curve. A good mentor can make a huge difference. A mentor demonstrates the professionalism required to be successful. A mentor can lead

you to discover the talent inside of you. Sometimes you just need to be told that you can do it. In online trading communities, experienced traders mentor new traders at times for a fee, but often for free. I personally mentor a few traders at a time, and of course, I myself did and still have a trading mentor. It is important to note though that mentorship does not work unless you are receptive, listen, and then put in the work necessary to adapt successfully.

You should find a mentor whose trading style fits with your personality. For example, if momentum trading is your favorite style, you're wasting your time talking to me.

Although I trade them from time to time, my style is really only for those who have an intraday swing day mentality. I mostly focus on VWAP and Support or Resistance trades.

Reflection and Review

By now, you may correctly think that trading psychology and self-discipline, a series of proven trading strategies, and excellent money and risk management are the essential elements of success in trading. But there is another element that ties all of your trading fundamentals together: record-keeping.

Keeping records of your trades will enable you to learn from your past success and failure experiences and make you a better trader. In fact, the most important and the most effective way to continuously improve as a trader is to keep a diary of your trades. There are many consistently profitable traders around the world, trading different markets with different methods, but they all have one thing in common: they keep excellent records of their trades. It is a very tedious and boring task; but it is also a very necessary task. Journal your trades daily. Make sure to include the following points in your trading journal:

1. Your physical well-being (lack of sleep, too much coffee, too much food the night before, etc.)

2. The time of the day you made the trade

3. The strategy you were anticipating

4. How you found the opportunity (from a scanner, a chatroom, etc.)

5. Quality of your entry (risk/reward)

6. Sizing/management of your trade (scaling in and out as planned)

7. Execution of exits (following profit targets or stop losses)

I personally take a screenshot from my screen (with a free software called Screenshot Captor) and journal my trades in my blog with that software. Please visit my blog to get some ideas on how to journal your trades. You do not have to follow my style, but you should find what works best for you because to be successful, you must journal your trades daily.

Mike Bellafiore, co-founder of SMB Capital (a proprietary trading firm in New York City), writes in his book One Good Trade that the professional traders at his firm video record all of their trades during the day. In their afternoon session they sit around their conference room tables, enjoy a lunch catered by the firm, review their trades and group-think about better ways to take your money. Trading is a full contact sport and anything less than your complete focus is disrespectful to the game and will certainly knock you out of the game. Profitable traders constantly evaluate their trading system. They make adjustments every month, every day, and even intraday.

New traders often ask me how to improve after a series of losses and a period of struggling. I recommend to them that they review their journal and look more specifically at what precisely they are doing poorly at in their trading. I am doing poorly doesn't mean anything. You cannot improve if you don't have a proper record of your daily trades.

Is it your stock selection? Is it your entry points?

Is it your discipline or psychology?

Is it your platform or clearing firm (broker)?

What about other traders, is it a bad month for everyone or just for you?

If the new trader lives in Vancouver, Canada, I usually meet them in person and identify the areas that need to be improved. If I cannot meet them in person, we have a chat over Skype and evaluate their performance. One time a trader complained about her order execution speed. I remotely connected to her PC (using TeamViewer, a remote control/remote access software) and evaluated the CPU performance.

I had to remove many unnecessary programs and apps from her PC, run a malware scanner and remove a variety of intrusive software, computer viruses, spyware, adware, scareware, and other malicious programs. I freed up a lot of the PC's memory and CPU capacity and her trading execution speed increased significantly. Your PC, just like your body and mind, needs to be kept clean, lean and fast, all of which have a direct effect on your trading platform and eventually your trading results.

I personally live video record all of my trades during the morning session (as I rarely make any trades Mid-day or at the Close). I believe traders, like athletes, should watch their trading videos. The best athletes and teams watch films of themselves to see what they're doing right and wrong, and how best to improve. I will review my tapes during Mid-day and make sure to note important observations on my entry, exit, price action, Level 2 signals and so on. I try to learn as much as possible from my trades.

Sometimes I look for new algorithmic programs that I must be aware of. I search for areas that I could have added more size. This is one of my trading weaknesses. I also do a poor job of holding for a longer time the stocks that are going in my favor. I therefore consider trades that I could have held longer. I make sure to find spots where I was too aggressive and to find trades that did not offer a good risk/reward opportunity but that I still took the trade in.

I review my position sizing and why and where I added more. That is How to Day Trade for a Living. There is no other way to get better. There are no excuses in trading. T o get better and to help traders in my community, I have to do this.

Watching trading videos also shows me how easy trading is when there are no emotions attached to a trade. When I review my work, I am not invested in a trade in real time with real money. Trading live, the market seems fast and unpredictable. When you watch back your trading video, you see that the market is actually very slow. There are times when I see the pattern in a stock by watching my video and recognize how I traded the stock backward, and that is embarrassing for someone of my experience.

I later review my videos over the weekend to create educational series to use in teaching day trading. Over the weekend, after I celebrate the winning week on Friday night with my friends and family in Vancouver, I lock myself into my home office and cut tape after tape to develop and update my training programs.

Watching your videos is an exercise that can benefit all traders no matter their experience. New traders need to watch the markets trade. Watching your videos increases your trading experience and confidence and significantly shortens your learning curve. But I agree, it takes time and it is indeed boring.

Chapter 14: Dispelling the Myths of Day Trading

As a trader that utilizes both short-term and day-trading strategies, I have been given a unique insight into the true benefits and disadvantages of both. As a teacher of trading, I have also had the opportunity to hear many oft quoted expressions in regard to trading that are firmly believed, but simply do not hold up under scrutiny. Many of these center on the subject of day-trading. If you are interested in day-trading, then it behooves you to know what is true and what is not.

Myth 1 - Day-trading is risky, much more than short-term trading or investing.

Without doubt, the risk is greater for short-term trading. In any single trade you are risking far less in a day-trade than in ether a short-term trade or long-term investment. What gives the appearance of greater risk is that you are typically taking more trades. Even on my worse day I have never lost as much as I have short-term trading.

Yes, that is right. Even on my worse day combining all of those day trades I still have not matched what I have lost with some of my short-term trades even though they are just one single trade. My own experience demonstrates that short-term trading and investing often proves riskier than day-trading. Surprised?

You shouldn't be, it is a matter of common sense. How much do you risk on a day trade as opposed to a short term trade? If a short-term trade has so much of a greater potential loss than any day trade what is going to be the naturally outcome when trades go bad?

Myth 2 - Day-trading is gambling

Any trading is gambling if you trade without a plan or allow emotion to control your decisions. The key difference is whether you are putting the odds in your favor or not. If you are doing so then the trading, whether you are talking about short-term, investing, or day-trading, becomes a business. If you can't put the odds in your favor then all of them can be considered gambling. None have an advantage over another.

Myth 3 - Day-trading ties you to a computer all day

I have to laugh at this myth. My typical day is an hour and a half in the morning and two hours in the afternoon, with a two hour lunch break. Even when I am trading I don't watch the market all the time because I am waiting for set ups to develop, so often I am playing a game on the computer or watching television while waiting. There are limited times when a market trends during the day, the most profitable times to trade. Most of the time it just consolidates.

During these down times when the market is in consolidation there is no need to watch the markets like a hawk. There are very simple ways to alert you when it is time to prepare for a trade. Frequent breaks should be the norm, not the rarity. I don't know of any other career that can pay you as much and yet give you so much free time.

Myth 4 - Day-trading is too stressful

Any trading is stressful if you are losing money, just as any trading is easy if you are making lots of profit. It isn't the type of trading, but how well you adapt to it and whether you are successful or not. The stress of day-trading typically results from two things; poor trading and the inability to adjust emotionally to the fast pace. Day-trading requires much faster responses because they are made in real time.

There isn't much time to analyze and then reanalyze a situation before making a decision like a person might do with short-term trades. So a trader needs to know their trading method well, to the point that it is almost second nature and they also need to keep their emotions in check.

While it may be difficult to initially do this, many of us have already mastered other endeavors that require real time critical decisions, such as driving an automobile. To acquire such ability is a simply matter of practice, practice and then more practice.

Myth 5 - The Biggest money is made on longer term moves lasting weeks or longer

A day-trader can double, triple, quadruple, and more beyond that of a person trading the longer term trend. This is because a market will naturally weave up and down as it develops, allowing for repeated profits covering the very same range. Having done both I know firsthand that a successful day-trader can blow away any short-term or long term investor when it comes to profits.

The only time a short-term trader will manage to make more profit is when a market gaps overnight, but even with this figured in a successful day-trader will usually be rewarded much more handsomely over the long term.

Myth 6 - When you day trade you miss out on the big profits generated by overnight gaps

You also miss out on the overnight losses as well. Gaps indicate high volatility and in many cases the market will swing violently both ways. Day-trading protects you from that overnight risk. But here is the surprising twist about overnight gaps; it is not uncommon for a market to close an overnight gap during the day, giving a day trader a chance to capture the profit generated by overnight trading anyway.

There are of course some markets that are not well suited for day-trading, while others are. So market choice can make a considerable difference when it comes to this issue. Trading a market that is inclined to overlap itself during the day will more than make up for any overnight gaps that occur.

While there are many more myths that could be dispelled here, it is also important to be balanced and consider the other side of the coin; the negative aspect of day-trading. While day-trading is a great way to make a living when you are consistently profitable, it can also be the worse career choice if you consistently lose. This is true of any type of trading, but in day-trading an individual typically has given up a regular job and of course, a regular income. Also, more is demanded emotionally.

This latter factor is one that most assume is personally of no concern and yet often proves to be the one issue preventing their success. There is an inherent weakness of emotion that everyone has and yet most refuse to believe they personally could have an issue with it. So they often fail to ever address it correctly and it continues to plague them.

However, if a trader does learn to trade profitably on a consistent basis and they also learn to control their emotions then day-trading is absolutely one of the greatest means for making a living that anyone can pursue. The freedom to work when you want to, the amount of money that can be made, and the lifestyle it provides is truly amazing. It really is all that is promised; the dream job. Although it takes a lot of work to reach that goal, do not be swayed by the myths about day-trading. This one is for real.

Conclusion

Now that you've reached this part of the book it's time to give yourself a pat on the shoulder. Throughout the course of this book, you've learned valuable information that will help you on your way to becoming a successful day trader. Now that you know what to do, the next and most important step is to put it into practice.

You can have the best trading strategy, the right mindset and attitude, but without practice you will be thrown into the pit unguarded. So after you've identified the trading strategy that suits you the most, it's now time to take action. Be confident in the things you have learned, follow your plan, and control your emotions. I wish you nothing but the best in your day trading journey.

-- **Leigh Vernon**

Dear Reader,

Thanks for exploring this book with me. Now that you know your way around the stock market...

...why not take one step further and understand the psychology behind trading?

You'll love the sequels to this book, because they all complement each other.

Get them now.

Thanks,

Leigh

P.S. Reviews are like giving a warm hug to your favorite author. We love hugs.

https://www.amazon.com/dp/B07GNTJ4C1

Check Out Other Books

DAY TRADING FOR A LIVING BOOK 2: Investing Psychology for Beginners

https://www.amazon.com/dp/B07J64GGKR

DAY TRADING FOR A LIVING BOOK 3: A Beginner's Guide to Forex

https://www.amazon.com/dp/B07K2Y8KN9

www.ingramcontent.com/pod-product-compliance
Lightning Source LLC
Chambersburg PA
CBHW070114230526
45472CB00004B/1259